From Eden to Nazareth

Finding Our Story
in the Old Testament

From Eden to Nazareth

Finding Our Story in the Old Testament

Leonard Foley, O.F.M.

Nihil Obstat:
> Rev. Hilarion Kistner, O.F.M.
> Rev. John J. Jennings

Imprimi Potest:
> Rev. Jeremy Harrington, O.F.M.
> Provincial

Imprimatur:
> + Daniel E. Pilarczyk
> Archdiocese of Cincinnati
> December 6, 1982

The *Nihil Obstat* and *Imprimatur* are a declaration that a book or pamphlet is considered to be free from doctrinal or moral error. It is not implied that those who have granted the *Nihil Obstat* and *Imprimatur* agree with the contents, opinions or statements expressed.

Book design, cover and illustrations by Julie Lonneman.

SBN 0-86716-020-9

Introduction

I don't think anybody reads introductions. They're usually about as exciting as the list of ingredients on your peanut butter jar. There's a sort of suspicion in people's minds, I think: If the title has caught my fancy, why not get started right away? Is the author so uncomfortable about the book that he or she has to ease me into it like a used-car salesman?

But publishers make us poor scribes write an introduction anyway, on the famous principle of the preacher who said, "First I tells 'em what I'm gonna tell 'em."

This book is about the Old Testament, and it has three purposes:

First, I want *to help the reader sense the present-day timeliness of the Story*. It's not out of date, because some things never change: God's loving pursuit of his children, his children's struggle with faith and fidelity, their lapses into sin and punishment, their reentry into mercy and grace.

Second, I have chosen *to highlight those parts of the Old Testament where this ever-old, ever-new pattern of grace, sin and redemption can be most clearly traced:* the creation and the fall; the forming of God's people in the fire of slavery and the miracle of the Exodus; the solemn covenant amid the thunder of Sinai; the glory of David's reign; the great tragedy of the Exile, seen through the tears of Jeremiah; the unquenchable hope of deliverance seen in the Book of Daniel. And I have included the story of Ruth—a small vase of roses in a family room that has seen both delight and degradation.

Third, I have tried *to pass on a little of what Bible scholars have discovered about the way the Bible was written*—or, rather, the *ways* the Bible was written. Its writers used many forms, as writers always do, to clothe their vision: stark narrative and the vehicle of fiction; poetry and satire, made-up teaching stories and dry lists of regulations; crude realism and delicate lyricism.

The Bible is an interpretation of what goes on between God and his people, not a mere tape recording of sounds in the desert. It is a memorial that captures the spirit and meaning of past events and puts us in the middle of those events as they happen today. It is a book that could have been written only by people of faith—even though sinful people of faith.

It is a book marked, as all books are, by the culture and customs and values of the time. We attempt to see through that cultural veil to the ongoing Story within.

Finally, this book is written for the kind of people I meet at adult education courses in parishes: people who want to "know more about the Bible" but who do not have the time to enter on formal courses of study. If they read this book, I suppose it will be in scattered moments of quiet between the persistent calls of duty or circumstance. I hope it will reassure them of God's presence in this hurly-burly—where he has been all through the Story.

Contents

1.

In the Beginning,
the Good God...

How would you like to have your religion based on a story like this?
Apsu (sweet water) marries Tiamat (salt water) and begets the gods
Lahmu and Lahamu. But Apsu and Tiamat are so irritated at the noisy
gatherings of their children (and then grandchildren) that they decide to
destroy them. A young god Ea discovers the plot and kills Apsu. Then
Tiamat creates an army of monsters to fight Ea and avenge her dead
husband. As she opens her jaws to devour Marduk, leader of the
opposition, he sends in winds to hold them open, then pierces her heart.
He splits her dead body like a shellfish into two parts: The upper he
makes into the heavens, the lower into the earth and underworld.

There's more, but you get the idea. Hardly a group likely to
inspire you to turn the other cheek.

The writers of Genesis, the first book of the Bible, knew stories
like this one from the pagans who lived around them. To some extent
they were affected by them. They accepted the "science" of their day,

describing a dome over the earth which holds up the waters above, etc. But they cleaned up the silly pagan accounts and gave us a God we can easily believe in today. With a few simple strokes the Jewish authors conveyed a whole system of religious truth.

So the reader's patience is asked as we separate the first few pages of the Bible into a four-part consideration: the Good God (Chapter 1); the Earthling, innocent image of God (Chapter 2); the Earthling turned sinner (Chapter 3); and what kind of book this is (Chapter 4).

The First Creation Story

The Bible begins (most of us don't notice) with two different stories of creation which simply ignore each other. In the second account, God acts like a human being. In the first, our concern for this chapter, God is the absolute master of creation, effortlessly producing a majestic universe.

Bible scholars name the writers of this first creation story (Genesis 1:1—2:4a) the "Priestly source," for reasons we will consider later. A later editor placed it at the beginning of the Bible as a fitting introduction—a majestic, sweeping picture of the transcendent God. He creates merely by his word; he is not subject to the crudeness and limitations of the pagan gods.

"God *said*"—and things happened. We scatter words as trees scatter leaves in autumn, but to the Semitic mind, the spoken word has a built-in power. It doesn't die when it leaves the lips and the sound fades away. In the Old Testament, "word" and "deed" are frequently one and the same thing.

So the constant repetition of "God said" is the same as to say "God did." The author's purpose is to show the supreme power and effortlessness of God's creating.

Genesis does not explain God. "In the beginning" of *our* time, God simply *is*. And God is *good;* therefore all creation is good. Seven times in 31 verses the Priestly author says, "God saw how good it was." Indeed, the seventh and final statement is "God looked at everything he had made, and he found it *very* good" (Genesis 1:31,* emphasis

---

* Unless otherwise noted, all Scripture citations in this chapter refer to the Book of Genesis.

added). God is infinitely superior to the quarreling, lusting, mindless deities of the pagans.

'Creation out of Nothing' or 'Order out of Chaos'?

Scripture scholars hold that the idea of "creation from nothing" was not an important consideration for the biblical authors. Their concern was for the beauty and goodness of what God created.

The word used in the first verse of the Bible, *bara* ("made," "created"), can mean creation from nothing. But we may be surprised if we look more closely: "In the beginning, *when* God created the heavens and the earth, *the earth was a formless wasteland,* and darkness covered the abyss, while a mighty wind swept over the waters" (1:1-2, emphasis added).

This primordial mess is generally described as "chaos." What did the Priestly author mean by the word? Certainly he did not mean that God first created the mess, then put order and beauty into it. Rather, one may guess, he expressed a profound truth: *Chaos is the alternative to God's good creation.* (And we have the terrible power to "create" it ourselves. A large part of the Bible is the story of our doing just this.) It is the nothingness into which we would collapse if God were to withdraw his sustaining power. It is the mess we fall into without God. Chaos is the evil that lurks behind all being. It is nothing to be afraid of, as long as we are in God's hands—but it is there: the possibility of evil, nothingness, darkness.

Some scholars see the wind that swept over the waters as the creating Spirit of God. Others point out that the Hebrew word for what the wind did ("swept") is parallel with the chaos already mentioned, and therefore probably has a similar "bad" meaning. It is the final brush stroke in a picture of disorder—the dark primordial waters whipped into a frenzy by a wind, chaos out of control.

Then God spoke and there was order.

In other words, the sacred author is saying that God's work is the total opposite of all that is grotesque or disordered or evil. He has lifted up his creation from nothingness and holds it there, and he will not let it down. God indeed has "got the whole world in his hands." Only one creature can plunge back into chaos—the thinking, conscious, free human being at the pinnacle of creation. (The swift descent to the babble of Babel takes only 11 chapters of Genesis.)

3

Light Without the Fourth-Day Sun

God spoke, and the darkness of chaos was bathed in light. Sometimes we're not very complimentary to the authors of the magnificent story of creation. We don't give them credit for seeing the obvious problem that every child reading Bible history immediately spots: How can you have light on the first day, when the sun and the moon are created only on the fourth day? The Priestly author was just as smart as we are: He obviously had another kind of "light" in mind.

The deeper meaning rests on the universal human instinct that light suggests goodness, beauty, peace, happiness and that darkness reminds us of evil, the unseen threat of danger. Light is not identified with God (as it is in 1 John 1:5) but is seen as a reflection and overflowing of the divine goodness. It comes first as the basis for everything else. Life is to be lived in God's light. The inspired author is saying that the world God made was good, orderly, beautiful, and that the foundation and base of all life is good. And "God saw how good the light was" (1:4).

The Six Days of Creation

In the Babylonian story, Marduk separated Tiamat's body into two spheres: the upper dome (the heavens) and the earth and underworld below. The Priestly author has adopted this literary device. God's first creating activity is three days of *separation:*

- On the first day God *separates* light and darkness.
- On the second day God *separates* the waters above the sky from the waters on the earth below.
- On the third day God *separates* earth and sea.

Then God spends three days *equipping* what he has made:

- On the fourth day God *equips* what he made on the first day. He furnishes the sky with sun, moon and stars.
- On the fifth day God equips what he made on the second day. He furnishes the waters below "with an abundance of living creatures." And beneath the waters above "birds fly beneath the dome of the sky" (see 1:20-21).
- On the sixth day God *equips* or furnishes the earth he made on the third day. He creates life on earth, "all kinds of wild animals, all kinds of cattle, and all kinds of creeping things" (1:25). Finally, God makes images of himself: conscious, free,

4

responsible creatures—human beings.

A bold position of the Priestly author may be lost on us here. At a time when most of humankind thought itself the slaves of the gods— among whom were sun, moon and stars *governing* human life— Genesis almost nonchalantly and offhandedly says that *God* made sun, moon and stars and they do not rule human life.

What has all this six-day scheme to do with creation vs. evolution? Nothing. The Priestly author is making a theological statement: The good God made the universe and all that is in it, and it is unbelievably beautiful. In our modern phrase, he "couldn't care less" whether God took a zillion years or did everything *zap,* just like that. (In the second story of creation, which we will consider in the next chapter, another author casts God in human form, has him walk in the cool of the evening, form the human body out of clay—obvious figures of speech. If they *aren't* figures of speech, then God would be just another Marduk or Tiamat.)

The Image of God

In this first creation story we must wait until verse 26 to meet a human being. Still, the Priestly author puts "him" at the pinnacle of creation. As the Psalmist would later sing,

> You have made him little less than the angels,
>   and crowned him with glory and honor.
> You have given him rule over the works of your hands,
>   putting all things under his feet....(Psalm 8:6-7)

After centuries of immersion in the Judeo-Christian heritage, we take our dignity so much for granted that we cannot appreciate the *boldness* of the words of Genesis:

> God created man in his image;
>   in the divine image he created him;
>   male and female he created them. (1:27)

How is man the image of God? First, the Priestly author is concerned with the creation of the whole human race. The full meaning of *man* is "male and female." Let me quote directly an author from whom I have borrowed heavily in this chapter, Father Bruce Vawter:

> The Priestly author is not describing the shaping of the human form

5

but the creation of the human species. There is no indication that he thought of one man only as the object of this creation or even of a single human pair. The contrary is suggested by the context into which he has inserted this story of creation—"all kinds" of wild animals, cattle, etc.—and also by the language of the story itself: *Let us make man...Let them have dominion...God created man...male and female he created them. (On Genesis,* p. 56)

The central emphasis in this opening chapter of the Bible is on *human dignity*. We are *image*. The word is no pale, halfhearted expression. It means, in Hebrew, an exact reproduction—precisely the kind of idol or image the Jews were forbidden to make or worship. The Priestly author is using a metaphor, of course, but it is as bold a comparison as can be imagined. (How terribly ironic that the first sin is an attempt to become like God!)

Today, after God's full revelation in Jesus, we know better the meaning of *image*. We are like God because we share his nature; we live in his life and with his life; we are in grace. Perhaps the Priestly author subconsciously suspected this, but we should not read the fullness of later revelation into the opening pages of Genesis.

Even from a purely human viewpoint, we can understand ourselves as images of God because we are gifted with intelligence and freedom. We can "look at ourselves," that is, reflect, be conscious, choose, understand.

Humankind is also like God in having dominion over nature. God said:

> "Be fertile and multiply; fill the earth and subdue it. Have dominion over the fish of the sea, the birds of the air, and all the living things that move on the earth." (1:28)

The human race is not the slave of the gods or the planets, but is destined to rule the earth.

The word for this dominion is the same one used to describe the authority of kings. But God's authority, unlike most earthly kings, is not only absolute but loving. To reflect his image faithfully, our domination must share God's love and respect for his holy creation.

The Seventh Day: God's 'Rest'

Why six days for creation? A good guess is that the original author compressed the narrative into six days to teach approval of the sabbath which follows the six-day work week. God rests like a good Jew and a good Jew rests like God. Remember, this narrative was written by the Priestly tradition; therefore it says that the one purpose of the sun, moon and stars is to mark the days—a liturgical purpose.

But, more deeply, the "rest" of God symbolizes the special relationship of peace and repose between the beautiful orderly world and its Creator. God blesses the sabbath day and, when his people observe it, they are made holy—set apart, as the seventh day was, by the Creator. On this day Israel enters, or reenters, its special relationship with God.

On God's part, this relationship is intended never to end: There is no morning or evening of the seventh day.

A Simple Story

It is easy to hurry through Genesis 1:1—2:4a, to call it naive and unsophisticated, perhaps a little childish and certainly not scientific. But ask yourself this question: In all the literature of the world, do you know any narrative that bears such weight of profound truth? Can you imagine any better way of teaching the world—educated and uneducated—the fundamental facts of its relation to the Creator?

After we have looked at the second story, we will try to summarize the basic religious teachings so purely expressed in these few verses at the beginning of our Bible.

7

2.
The *Adam*,
Beloved of God

The Bible starts over in the second chapter of Genesis. Suddenly we are reading an entirely new story of creation (2:4b-25) that simply ignores the first chapter. The majestic sweep of the Priestly author's account has indeed provided a solemn, almost liturgical introduction to the Bible, but now we have left the Temple and taken our place at the campfire where a wonderful storyteller holds our attention.

Bible scholars have named this storyteller "the Yahwist" because Yahweh is the name he uses for God. This author's primary interest is humanity; even the Lord Yahweh he presents is described in human terms. His God molds clay with his hands, walks in the garden, etc.

In the second account God has, as it were, held up creation until he is ready to make man. There was no shrub or grass "because the LORD God had sent no rain upon the earth and there was no man to till the soil" (Genesis 2:5). Notice that again the *how* of creation is of little or no interest to the writer. God made it all, somewhere back there.

9

Now comes the important climax: humanity. What God needs now is some good wet water so that he can make clay from the dust and produce *adam* (the "earthling") from the *adama* (earth, ground).

What's in a Name?

Let's stop here a moment and consider "Adam" and "adam." The Yahwist will tell the story of creation by setting before us a typical couple who are merely called the man and the woman. He is not talking about a particular couple, but is concerned with describing the creation of humanity in general.

But let's not make inexact statements. It sometimes happens, after people have taken a Bible course, that they say (to the horror of others) that "there wasn't any Adam." That's not true. There was *adam*, humanity. However creation happened, we can suppose that someone was the first human being, just as someone was the first Italian. But the point the author is trying to make is simple: It was the good God who made human beings, and he made them out of love.

The Breath of Life

The Yahwist's God, as we have said, is given human characteristics. He has to mold the earthling from clay like a potter. He lifts it to his mouth (as in modern mouth-to-mouth resuscitation) and "blows" the breath of life into the body's nostrils.

Some scholars hold that this breath is a special kind of life that comes from God, distinguishing humanity from all other creatures. Others say it is no different from the life God gives to all living beings. Gloomy Qoheleth writes:

> For the lot of man and beast is one lot; the one dies as well as the other. Both have the same life-breath, and man has no advantage over the beast; but all is vanity. (Ecclesiastes 3:19)

The Yahwist himself has not yet distinguished the *adam* from the other animals, though he will later in the story when a suitable partner is sought for this new creature.

A digression here: We *now* know, from the fullness of revelation, that God does "blow" a very special kind of life—the sharing in his own life which we call grace—into all who open themselves to his coming. This is the refined fullness of revealed truth. The writers of

Genesis—and indeed the whole Old Testament—did not necessarily have this awareness. It took time for God to bring his people along (it still does) from a very primitive morality (or immorality) to the perfect revelation of his will in Jesus. So we must neither be shocked at the pessimism of Qoheleth nor drawn into reading more into the early books of the Bible than was necessarily in the minds of the writers.

The Yahwist is certain of one thing: The *adam,* the earthling, is the center of Yahweh's universe. The rest of creation is for him. Its details are unimportant; the storyteller mentions only the garden that God provided "in Eden, in the East" (2:8*). There Yahweh planted trees for the man's enjoyment, "delightful to look at" and, secondarily, "good for food" (2:9). Fertility is assured by the great river which rises to water the garden and divides into four tributaries, including the Tigris and the Euphrates of present-day Iraq (see 2:10-14).

Yahweh settles the human he has made into the garden, giving it into his care with one caution: The man may eat of any tree in the garden but one, the tree of knowledge of good and evil. "From that tree you shall not eat; the moment you eat from it you are surely doomed to die" (2:17). For just a moment a shadow flickers over Eden.

A Suitable Partner

The Yahwist now comes to the distinction—and equality—of the sexes. First he emphasizes the fact that God created humanity. Now he speaks of God's creation as a typical individual *male,* and implies that humanity is incomplete if it is only male, masculine.

God creates "partners" for the earthling: animals and birds. He brings them to the earthling, who names them. This means much more than merely pasting labels on them. It makes sense to call a hippopotamus a "river horse" but what does it mean to call a horse a horse? In the biblical sense, it means power. To name something is to know all about it and be able to control it, use it. (To this day, some Arabs will not let you write their name on a piece of paper: "My name is *me!"*) The Yahwist's emphasis is on the man's superiority to all other beings, his dominance over creation.

But none of these is "a suitable partner" (2:20). The Yahwist now

---

* Unless otherwise noted, all Scripture citations in this chapter refer to the Book of Genesis.

11

uses a word found elsewhere in the Bible for a sleep induced by God for his own purposes, during which he does marvelous things (see 1 Samuel 26:12; Isaiah 29:10; Genesis 15:12).

The marvelous thing God does is to make *wo-man* (Old English for female human). The Yahwist borrows from the literature of his day and has God make woman out of one of man's ribs, possibly a reference to a Sumerian symbol that can mean either "life" or "rib."

Now we no longer have the general name *adam* (the human being, the earthling) from *adama* (earth), but *ish* (the male) and *ishshah* (the female). The woman is called thus because she has been taken from ishah, the male—that is, she is of the same substance as he. There are still no personal names. Not until the next biblical chapter will we hear of "Eve"; not until the end of Genesis 4 is "Adam" used as a proper name. "At last," the man says,

> "This one…is bone of my bones
> and flesh of my flesh." (2:23)

She is a suitable partner, his only peer in creation.

"That is why"—because the female is the complement of the male, his equal, his peer—"a man leaves his father and mother and clings to his wife, and the two of them become one body" (2:24). Actually, Hebrew has no word for "body" as we understand it, only "flesh," which means a person's whole being, identity, heart and soul and body combined.

So we have a perfect picture of marriage as God made it: The total, personal, heart/soul/body union of man and woman together make a new "person."

The man and the woman are both naked, yet they feel no shame. They romp like bare-skinned toddlers under the eye of an all-loving, approving parent, still unaware of their own power to overstep the bounds of safety and happiness. The Yahwist is leading up to the first sin, but first he must add this last touch of innocence, the finishing stroke to an idyllic scene, as a reminder of the goodness of God's creation.

3.
Sin:
'You Will Be Like Gods!'

Back in the first creation account, the Priestly author reminded us that there is an alternative to God's creation: chaos. And now it breaks through—not of itself, but by the deliberate choice of the free, intelligent beings God placed at the pinnacle of creation.

We blithely define this chaos, evil, as the absence of good: Sickness is the absence of health; hate is the absence of love; greed is the absence of justice, etc. But goodness gets a little boring. Who wants to read about the man who loves his wife, takes his kids to the zoo, keeps his grass cut and goes to church every Sunday?

Now the man next door, he's selling marijuana. Wouldn't you like to try it—just once? We are titillated by the nothingness, the chaos. Evil has a certain fascination. As the Music Man sang, "I smile, I grin, when the gal with the touch of sin walks in." Evidently this itch is not only the *result* of sin (concupiscence, the catechism called it) but somehow also its *cause*.

The Yahwist, continuing his story under God's inspiration, describes this fatal human itch with a brilliant psychological picture (Genesis 3*) that stands in terrible contrast to the two "innocent" chapters with which the Bible began.

The *serpent* enters the garden. Why did the Yahwist pick this creature? Why not a rat, or a pig, or a vulture? Because the serpent was seen as *cunning*, a fitting symbol of the deceptive nature of evil. The serpent also played a role in pagan fertility rites—a clear association with evil in the storyteller's eyes. Later generations named the devil as the great instigator of all evil, but the Yahwist apparently wanted only to show the clever deceptiveness that leads us through the beckoning curtains of sin.

The serpent's opening gambit: "Did God *really* tell you not to eat from *any* of the trees in the garden?" (3:1, emphasis added). ("Don't tell me you're not allowed!") The woman (alas, the Yahwist was probably a man, or the whole story might have had a reversal of roles!) protests her freedom, but adds a pouty little touch of resentment: "It is only about the fruit of the tree in the middle of the garden that God said, 'You must not eat it *or even touch it,* lest you die'" (3:3, emphasis added).

Note that both the serpent and the woman misquote God. The order God had given was,

> "You are free to eat from any of trees of the garden except the tree of knowledge of good and bad. From that tree you shall not eat; the moment you eat from it you are surely doomed to die." (2:16-17)

Not "any tree," as the serpent taunted, or "not even touch," as the woman pouted. Sin must always hide or distort part of the truth.

"Lest you die? Not so, my dear. It is not certain that you will die. Actually, God is afraid you are going to be like gods, who know what is good and what is bad." A strange temptation for one who is already, in the Priestly author's account, the very image of God!

The serpent's assertion retains a hint of pagan stories in which gods and goddesses are very jealous of their special prerogatives— knowledge, immortality—in the face of threatened human invasion.

---

* Unless otherwise noted, all Scripture citations in this chapter refer to the Book of Genesis.

But the Yahwist's concern is the *human* flaw. He is saying there is something which is beyond the control of creatures, something that it is not proper for them to aspire to. There is some "godness" that is the source of their being, something they must adore, submit to, depend on.

The woman lets herself be flattered by the delicious prospect of independence. Why shouldn't we revel in knowing everything, deciding everything for ourselves? Who wants to be a slave, dependent, obedient? She could see for herself that the tree was "good for food, pleasing to the eyes, and desirable for gaining wisdom" (3:6).

She decides. She chooses three good things—food, beauty, "wisdom"—which have swollen in importance in her imagination and crowded out the basic good of her life —simple loving *acceptance* of God and his word. We never choose evil as such; we choose good over greater good.

Now they are ashamed in the presence of God as he walks in the garden. They have "matured" ("The following program is for mature audiences only.") at the price of innocence. "Then the eyes of both of them were opened, and they realized that they were naked" (3:7). They have tasted the nothingness of evil, and something has gone out of them—some wholeness, some total personal health and well-being. The Yahwist uses their bodily shame—not in itself a sign of evil—as a symbol of their self-humiliation, stupidity and freely-chosen sin.

Now begins another very typically human process. The master psychologist-author writes a story that has been repeated a million times. The man admits that he ate, but implies that it is partly *God's* fault for giving him this woman! "The woman whom you put here with me—she gave me fruit from the tree, *and so* I ate it" (3:12, emphasis added). The woman passes the blame on: "The serpent tricked me into it" (3:12).

Symbols of Punishment

The *serpent* is punished first. The Yahwist uses its natural characteristics (crawling, "eating dust") as symbols of its degradation.

There will, God says, be a permanent war between the human race (the collective seed of the woman) and the powers of evil (the collective seed of the serpent). The same word is used for what they will do to each other: *crush*. Since this section concerns punishment, it

16

is unlikely that the author had in mind what Christian faith later perceived: a promise of victory by Jesus, the seed of Mary over the devil, the seed of the serpent.

We can, as we read the Bible, see the story of the promised Jesus in the whole history of God's dealing with his children: God knew what he would do; Jesus is the firstborn of all creation, the center of history. All history finds its resolution in his life-giving death and resurrection. Hence the view of faith can traditionally call Genesis 3:15 the *protoevangelium,* the "first Gospel."

But the first way to read the Bible is to take the meaning the author consciously intended, as is evident from his style, the form of writing he chooses, the culture of the time, etc. Read in this way, these verses speak only to perpetual human struggle with evil; more than half the Fathers of the Church did not consider their message messianic. There's nothing to be regretted about this: Wishful thinking doesn't help truth.

Next, God turns to the woman. The harsh lot of woman in the ancient world is used as a symbol of her punishment—the fact that she bore her children in pain, and that she was drawn to her husband but found him to be a master rather than an equal companion.

> Note that these words are not a curse, and far less are the pains of childbirth represented as the divinely ordained destiny for woman. Like disease and other physical evils, they are the result of sin, and like disease they may be alleviated without scruple. (*A New Catholic Commentary on Holy Scripture,* p. 180).

The difficulty with which man now wrests food from the earth is the symbol of his punishment. Creation will no longer be peacefully cooperative with him.

Finally will come *death.* Human beings extinguished the life of humble acceptance in their heart, and their earthly life was thereby doomed to wither away—a symbol of being what St. Paul calls "flesh," that is, attempting to be independent and falling under the weight of ultimate human helplessness.

Beyond Eden

So far the Yahwist has been describing beings in general—what they *typically* are. These typical human beings he individualizes—a man and a woman. Now suddenly the woman has a name: *Eve*. "The man called his wife Eve because she became the mother of all the living" (3:20). The word in Hebrew resembles another word for "life." ("Adam," as we have seen, is not, at first, the individual name of one man, but a general description of those taken from the earth, *adama*.)

The tragedy of humankind is now apparently permanent. Cherubim and a fiery revolving sword keep the fallen from ever again enjoying the garden, where the tree of life would have been a permanent source of happiness.

From now on—the rest of the first 11 chapters of Genesis—it is a plunge downhill. The estrangement and unhappiness of the sinful human race surfaces again and again: the murderer Cain (4:1-16), the flood (6:5—8:22) and, finally, the Tower of Babel—"the tower with its top in the sky"—the symbol of human arrogance in the face of God (11:9).

The human race has fallen into what was once described as foreign to its nature: "It is not good for the man to be alone" (2:18). Now, so self-centered that language is confused, people cannot understand one another. The words Milton put on Satan's lips are fittingly on the *adam's:* "Myself am hell."

4.
What Kind of Book Is This, Anyway?

The book of Genesis is a special kind of writing, and we must deal with that fact first. It was written by a people with a unique understanding of God and of God's role in their history: the people of Israel. Its authors, as we have seen in the previous chapters, were not concerned with the *how* of creation; they wanted to explain the beginnings of the world in light of their experience of God. In other words, they were interested in conveying the *truth* without having at hand very many *facts*.

Let's try a comparison to straighten out that confusion, keeping in mind that all similes limp and our parable may not present an exact picture. Let us suppose that you have the gift of words, and you want to put your mother and dad on paper—a memorial for your brothers and sisters and them only. Not the dead facts about what your parents' first house cost, or what train they took on their honeymoon, but the *feel* of their lives—the richness of their love, the spirit that moved beneath the

19

laughter and struggle and pain.

Suppose, further, that you want to write a chapter on the first year of their marriage. You weren't there, you've forgotten much of what they said about it, and you have just a few absolute facts—they were married in St. Martin Church, they lived on Elm Street, your sister Emily was born a year after they were married—and a deep and certain understanding of the *kind* of people they were.

You start with facts, and you put flesh on them from your authentic personal knowledge of them. As an artist with words, you create a piece of writing that really carries the basic facts and meaning of their lives, the flavor of what must have been. It's not a "made up" story, but a real story; only the literary form, or vehicle, of the story is made up.

Now, your art may lead you to construct a *typical* Sunday in their lives. Like this: "They had Wheaties and cream in the little sun-porch, and laughed at the mother robin trying to stuff a worm into a fledgling's mouth. [Actually, they may have had bacon and eggs in the kitchen.] They walked to church, holding hands. [In fact, maybe they drove, with your mother scrunched close to your dad.] They read the Sunday paper sprawled on the living room rug, trading choice bits of news or ads. [Actually, they may not have subscribed to a newspaper, and spent most of Sunday afternoon working in the garden.]"

What you are writing is true to their character, and it rests on truths you are absolutely sure of: marriage, love, sacrament, faithfulness, humor, faith, etc. You avoid anything that would contradict what you know about the kind of people your parents were.

A Family History

This long-winded introduction seems necessary to help us approach the first chapters of Genesis on their own terms. No part of the Bible can really be understood without a careful examination as to the kind of writing involved in any one book: narrative, fiction, poetry, teaching stories, drama, prayers, etc. And the beginning of Genesis is very much like your account of your parents' first year.

First, the descriptions of creation were written *only for those who believed*, those who were "in on" the Jewish view of life—just as your account was for family consumption only. Strangers would get only a glimmering of what you were talking about, but your brothers and sisters would get your meaning right away and enjoy the authentic picture. And nobody in your family would care whether it was gardening or swimming or watching TV they did on that Sunday. You wouldn't try to prove anything in a court of law from your poetic/ authentic account. So also we can't use the Bible to argue with people who aren't "of the family."

Secondly, the Bible's description of creation was written for believing Jews millions of years *after it happened*. Genesis was probably first put into writing about 500 B.C. The story of the world's beginning was included as a sort of introduction to the Story that was really of interest to the Jews: their own special history, which begins with Abraham.

If you ask, then, whether or not this is history, the answer is yes. If you ask *how* it is history, the answer is that it is history embodied in poetry, fiction, narrative, drama and many figures of speech. If you object that real events are mingled with made-up elements (six days, serpent, tree of life, etc.), then you must also ask yourself whether your account of your parents' first year was a true and authentic account of the character and meaning of *what* happened that year, no matter *how* it happened.

So, precisely because we recognize the non-historical framework and imagery of the beginning of the Bible, we are able to take it seriously as history.

How Genesis Came to Be

Although, scholars believe, nothing of Genesis existed in written form before around 500 B.C., it had long been told in oral tradition. Over hundreds of years, around campfires and water holes, poets and sages polished the story—the pre-story of the Chosen People (Creation and the Fall) and then the special promise, the choice of Israel as God's people. The accounts were statements of faith, not neutral, "value-free" sets of mere facts.

When, at different times and in different places, the stories were first written down, they included some materials that existed before Israel and probably came from northern Mesopotamia: pieces of myth, legend, saga, poetry. The authors kept some pagan elements (the dome which separates the waters, etc.) but used their own faith and theology to give meaning to the stories.

21

Scholars, by comparing such things as literary style, use of words, overall mood, emphasis, have identified four different kinds of writing in Genesis. We noted in Chapter 1 that the first creation story was written by what is called the "Priestly source" (P). This source, the same scholars tell us, had a tendency to put order and system into other authors' writings. Naturally, priestly interests are dominant. As we have already seen, the first creation story has overtones of liturgy and ritual. The P source developed over a long period of time, and around 450 B.C. was combined with the J, E, and D sources.

In contrast, the "Yahwist" (J—from the German word *Jahwist*) is, as we saw in Chapter 2, a colorful and imaginative writer. This tradition is thought to have flourished around about 1000-900 B.C., at a time when Israel was in its glory.

The Yahwist's God is the universal God of all, whether the Gentiles know this or not. The Jews are the Chosen—not a superior race, but an example of what God can do if he wants to.

We will meet a third source, E (the "Elohist," whose name for God is *Elohim*), in Chapter 6. The fourth source, D (Deuteronomic) is primarily concerned with the Law as Israel's loyal response to God's loving call. Though it includes some narrative, it did not contribute significantly to the books of the Bible we are considering in this volume.

A final editor gave the Old Testament its present form, skillfully fitting together pieces from the four traditions. This probably happened during the Exile, 587-583 B.C. (see Chapter 11).

What's This About Myth?

As we have seen, the Priestly author didn't concern himself with the creation of individuals at all, only the sweeping "male and female"—the whole human race. The Yahwist pictured *typical* individuals, just as you created a typical day in your parents' life: one pair of human beings, male and female. The Yahwist account begins the story of Everyman. One man and one woman are presented as doing what many did—and still do. The story of one sin is used to explain human sinfulness—a device scholars call *myth*.

Greek mythology is filled with gods and goddesses who never lived. Maybe the Greeks thought they did, but we don't. Hence the word *myth* means, primarily and for most people, what Webster defines as: "a person or thing having only an imaginary or unverifiable existence."

But what about your account of your parents' first year? You had only a few facts to go on but lots of experience, and your brothers and sisters all say your account is really true to life. It's really your father and mother. *You have created a myth.* Not something "imaginary and unverifiable," however. You have put flesh on some real events you did not witness. What you say about your parents is *typically true* and rests on a real marriage, a real home. This explains the second meaning of *myth,* the sense in which we can speak of the "Genesis myth."

For Jews, the Genesis myth was an attempt to put faith in concrete story form. These things really happened, in some way. Their meaning, moreover, is absolutely certain. The creation stories are myths in this second sense.

Let's stop here, again, and consider a loose way of talking about the Bible. Just as it isn't exact to say there wasn't any Adam, so it is not true to say that the first chapters of the Bible are "made up" stories (with the hint that perhaps the whole Bible is that way).

Creation, the event, the happening, is not made up. The meaning is not made up. The truths Genesis contains are not made up. What is made up is the medium, the vehicle, the flesh that carries the events and meanings. The Civil War really happened; the novel *The Red Badge of Courage* is one way (medium) to tell what happened, and to emphasize a fundamental meaning of the war. A culture other than Israel— suppose God had picked the Persians—might have used a different medium. But the facts and meaning would be the same.

Israel's historians used all kinds of material—ancient creation stories, genealogical lists, songs, proverbs, legends—as the material or framework of their myth. But they used these for their own theological purpose.

The basic question is, always: What did they *mean*?

The Truth of Genesis

The primary fact of Genesis is the Jewish experience of God's creative and redeeming love. A certainty acquired eons after creation, it is independent of the materials and forms used to carry the story. Compare again your version of your parents' marriage.

From the Jewish experience of the good and saving God, the

Genesis account presents an array of rock-bottom facts of faith:

- God is supreme in power; there are no rival gods.
- God is good, not the source of evil.
- God created the world at the beginning of time.
- All things are good.
- God made a special creation called humanity.
- Human beings are made in the image of God.
- The human race was created for friendship with God.
- Human beings are in charge of the earth as stewards of God.
- Evil entered the world through free human choice.
- Sin brings its wages of punishment and misery.
- The body is good.
- Male and female are equal.
- Marriage is meant to be monogamous.

Probably the list could be extended. Now, ask yourself this question: Suppose you wanted to teach these truths to a semi-developed people who had no books—or rather, to put into words, into an easily understandable and memorable story, what they already believed (in our analogy, what you and your brothers and sisters already knew about your parents). Can you think of a better vehicle, a more simple, true-to-life, easily understood story than that with which the Bible begins? Try to make up a better one, which will convey all the elements listed above. Try, besides, to use the only literary *forms* you know—the nonsense-filled story-forms of your pagan neighbors.

The more you think about it, the more you are amazed at the genius involved in those "naive" and "primitive" stories at the beginning of the Bible!

Those who are nervous about this account of how Genesis was written will do well to note what the Pontifical Biblical Commission in Rome (not known for rash and avant-garde statements) said as far back as 1948: 1) The early chapters of the Bible relate *truths presupposed* for the history of God's saving actions. 2) They do this in simple and *figurative language* adapted to the mentality of a less-developed people. 3) They are a *popular* description of the origin of the human race and of the Chosen People (see *Letter to Cardinal Suhard*, Jan. 16, 1948).

It doesn't matter that the writers build upon the obviously incorrect Babylonian science of their day. The point is that the "dome," the "waters above and below" are God's good creation, lovingly offered to humanity and totally under God's control.

God Has a Plan

The Jews did not, like their pagan neighbors, see the world as a plaything of the gods, but as a stage on which God was working out a definite plan of salvation. We might say that the word *salvation* is the most important one in the human vocabulary—with "God is love" as the counterbalance. The rather prosaic term "salvation history" means that history is moving toward a definite goal which God has in mind and which he will achieve.

Sometimes, the Bible goes on to record, God intervenes in a very direct way, without violating the freedom he gave his children. Persians and Greeks and Romans may grind these children into the dust, but God will lift them up. They may plunge themselves into Babel, but God will restore their speech. Assyrians may cart them off into exile, but God will bring them back. The world may seem the captive of sin and misery, but God promises—and sends—a Savior.

This is the story that begins in Genesis. Genesis tells of a good start and what looked like a bad ending. It slides from Paradise to Babel in 11 chapters. Now the Bible begins the long, painful journey up from the depth of human misery and sin. God calls Abraham, whose seed will be Jesus.

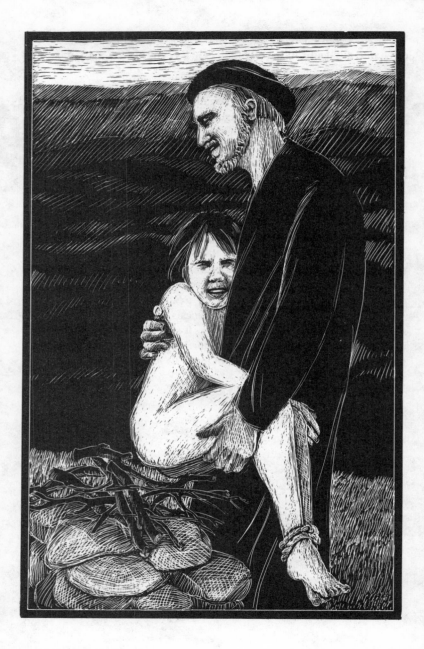

5.
Abraham:
The World Starts Over

The man looked down at the sleeping boy. He leaned over to
touch his cheek, then held back. It was already first light, and the
command must be swiftly obeyed. But just a few moments to look at
the smooth, peaceful face...

Isaac. The name meant that somebody laughed: Sarah perhaps, at
the preposterous promise that she would have a baby at her advanced
age; perhaps her friends, in ribald humor at her condition or rejoicing
with her at the blessing of God; or perhaps God himself, for the name
can mean, "May God smile."

The sleeping child was proof that God keeps his promise, the
seed of Abraham that would continue his line. Through this boy,
Abraham would become the father of thousands, ultimately the
benefactor of all nations. In his old age, Abraham had received an
unbelievable gift, a son whom he loved.

Long before this morning God called Abraham to pull up stakes and move out of his native land:

> The LORD said to Abram: "Go forth from the land of your kinsfolk and
> from your father's house to a land that I will show you.
> "I will make of you a great nation,
>   and I will bless you." (Genesis 12:1-2)

There aren't many occasions when the whole course of life turns
on the decision of one moment—to go east or west, to sign or tear up
the contract. That moment is made ready, of course, by a thousand
ripening moments of decision before it. But there is one crossroads that
is fateful for the whole. There are even fewer moments when the whole
course of history hangs on one decision. This was one of those critical
moments—like the angel's visit to Mary or Jesus' agony in Gethsemane
or the earthlings' longing look at the tree in the garden. This was the
beginning of God's plan to lift the world back out of the chaos into
which the earthlings' sin had plunged it.

The Bible, capturing this historic moment, is laconic:

> Abraham went as the LORD directed him. (Genesis 12:4)

He packed all his furniture and pots and pans and threw them on the
camels and moved out. He didn't go far, as we measure travel today
(about 400 miles). But if you've ever been homesick in a foreign
country where you're "stuck" for only God knows how long (I have
been), then you can sympathize with this first great sacrifice of
Abraham.

Abraham left Haran, at the age of 75, with many possessions. He
made the horseshoe turn around the Syrian desert and went down to
Shechem, in Canaan—someday to be the "Promised Land," but now a
stronghold of pagans. Religious man that he was, he immediately built
an altar there to the Lord; then he moved to a place near Bethel where
he built another altar and invoked the Lord by name—Mother Teresa
setting up shop next to the Kremlin. A famine drove him down to Egypt
for a while; then he returned to Bethel and finally settled at Hebron.

'Our Father in Faith'

St. Paul spent a large part of his Christian life arguing with
people who thought they could save their own souls by carrying out
(implicitly, by their own strength) all 613 percepts of the Law. His

great model—and argument—for the opposite attitude was Abraham, who let God cut him loose from his roots.

> "Abraham *believed* God, and it was credited to him as justice [holiness]." Now, when a man works, his wages are not regarded as a favor but as his due. But when a man does nothing, yet *believes* in him who justifies the sinful, his faith is credited to him as justice [holiness]. (Romans 4:3-5, emphasis added)

In other words, Abraham did not *earn* the favor (grace) of God, he *accepted* it.

Abraham didn't arrive at this attitude all at once, of course, and he may have wavered at times, as we all do. He too "laughed" about begetting a child in his old age. But he passed the test, substantially. (A passing grade may not be glorious, and good students aren't satisfied with that, but it *is* passing.) He made a great act of faith in God's promise that Isaac would even *exist*.

> Hoping against hope, Abraham believed and so became the father of many nations....Without growing weak in faith he thought of his own body, which was as good as dead (for he was nearly a hundred years old) and of the dead womb of Sarah. Yet he never questioned or doubted God's promise;...fully persuaded that God could do whatever he promised. (Romans 4:18-21)

It happened like this: God came to Abraham in a vision and promised him a very great reward. Abraham responded, "What good will it be, since I am childless?" Then God made the first promise of Isaac:

> "Your own issue [not one of your servants] will be your heir." He took him outside and said, "Look up at the sky and count the stars, if you can. Just so," he added, "shall your descendants be." Abraham put his faith in the LORD, who credited it to him as an act of righteousness. (Genesis 15:4-6)

More material for Paul's pulpit-pounding. And God not only promises, he makes or "cuts" a covenant.

They had some great liturgies in the old days: Moses throwing blood on the worshipers (see Exodus 24:6-8), Elijah calling down fire to consume the bulls of Baal (see 1 Kings 18:25-39). Abraham went through one too, when God made a covenant with him and sealed it with a terrifying ceremony that clearly shows faith is a life-and-death decision, not a tentative entry into the local tennis tournament.

At God's command, Abraham prepared a sacrifice: a heifer, a she-goat and a ram, a turtledove and a young pigeon. The bodies of the larger animals he cut in two, placing the halves opposite each other. Birds of prey, representing the threats to the covenant, swooped down on the carcasses, but Abraham stood his ground. (In Israel's subsequent history the birds often seem to succeed, but this night they are driven off by Abraham's faith.)

As the sun went down, Abraham fell into a trance and "a deep terrifying darkness enveloped him" (Genesis 15:12). Entering into the presence of God is running into the arms of a loving Father; it is also venturing into—or being allowed to enter—the court of the mysterious and awesome God.

When it got dark, a flaming torch and a smoking brazier—Old Testament signs of God's presence—appeared and passed between the pieces. Jeremiah (34:18) tells us the meaning of this symbolic action: It indicates the willingness of the contracting parties to suffer the same fate as the animals should they break the covenant.

In this case, God alone passes between the bodies. This covenant is one-sided: God is the only real "partner." Abraham is the creature who has nothing to give, who can only receive. He is the totally dependent *adam*. God repeats the promise: "To your descendants I give this land" (Genesis 15:18). Abraham has put his faith in a promise that cannot naturally be fulfilled—the birth of a child to a couple long past childbearing age. The relationship of trust and dependency between creature and Creator has been restored and celebrated in a stirring liturgy.

Test of Faith

But now, only a handful of years later, God has spoken again. A sudden, searing command this time:

> "Take your son Isaac, your only one, whom you love, and go to the land of Moriah. There you shall offer him up as a holocaust on a height that I will point out to you." (Genesis 22:2)

Abraham, who had shrewdly bargained with God about Sodom and Gomorrah (see Genesis 18:16-33), passed the test. Not a word passes his lips. The next sentence is coldly narrative:

30

> Early the next morning Abraham saddled his donkey, took with him
> his son Isaac, and two of his servants as well, and with the wood he
> had cut for the holocaust, set out for the place of which God had told
> him. (Genesis 22:3)

Gently Abraham shook the sleeping boy awake. In the early
morning light, the shock of the demand choked him. Mad thoughts
whirled through his mind. What kind of God was this, that would put
this tender gift in his arms and then tear it away, food for a fire? He
swallowed his agony, explaining nothing to his servants or to Isaac.
They trudged over the shimmering desert floor, the man's face streaked
with tears, the child blissfully following, the servants stolidly
husbanding their strength.

Three days into the heat and dust, Abraham saw the mountain.
He told the servants to stay behind, still dreading to tell them the truth.
He and the boy, Abraham told them, would worship and then come
back.

Father and son went up the mountain. Abraham carried the fire
and the knife; he laid the wood for the holocaust on Isaac's shoulders.
The young mind saw the problem right away. "Where is the sheep for
the holocaust?"

"God will provide." Was it a statement or a prayer or a wild
hope?

> When they came to the place of which God had told him, Abraham
> built an altar there and arranged the wood on it. Next he tied up his
> son Isaac, and put him on top of the wood on the altar. Then he
> reached out and took the knife to slaughter his son. (Genesis 22:9-10)

Notice how the biblical author hurries to get the scene over with,
and almost manages to make it sound routine. How many mothers and
fathers have paused here to reflect—ignoring the happy ending—on
what *they* would have done? How do you suddenly grab your child and
begin the tangled confinement of his arms and legs, as you breathe
fiercely and make your ears ignore his screams?

The horror is unthinkable, we say, as we try not to get callous
about abortion statistics. And it is precisely this unthinkableness that
may have been at least a secondary purpose of the story. Infant sacrifice
was common among the pagans; archeologists are constantly finding
infant skeletons buried under the thresholds of Canaanite homes and

31

city gates. The Abraham story may have been aimed at showing God's rejection of this kind of offering.

A Matter of Trust

But the point of the story is that, on the one hand, *God is absolutely sovereign* and that, on the other, *the creature is absolutely dependent*. This puts the case in its coldest, grimmest form—no happy ending necessarily promised.

We are conditioned to expect and demand personal rights in a democratic society. This attitude often expands to an exasperated questioning of God: "How can a good God allow the suffering of babies, the slaughter of millions?" It may even have another nuance: "How *dare* God treat me this way?"

At the risk of chilling our hearts for a moment or two, let's face this naked central truth: God is not our president, subject to laws, press conferences and even impeachment. He is not even like our human parents, who ultimately have no power or control over us. God is not a pal or a pope with whom one may argue intimately or in full court (though the Bible shows the Jews doing this all the time).

God is absolute being. He is absolute power. "Absolute" must not be divorced from "infinitely loving" and "kindhearted beyond all measure," but it must not be submerged beneath these ideas either.

Can God then, be unreasonable? It will seem so from our viewpoint, which can capture only a tiny area of human history—and that only from the outside. We have only a glimmering of the divine mind and heart. The glimmering is reassuring. An infinitely perfect and loving God cannot, in any event of our lives, be anything but the One described by the prophet:

> Can a mother forget her infant,
>> be without tenderness for the child of her womb?
> Even should she forget,
>> I will never forget you. (Isaiah 49:15)

What then? The only alternative to despair—for Abraham or for us—is *trust that rests on faith*. Faith the granite foundation, trust the warm home resting on it.

To put it most drily, faith is absolute commitment to God. It is inseparable from love, but it is not the same thing. As the song says,

32

you can't have one without the other. It is the act of putting our lives on the line (or, more starkly, on that stone altar of sacrifice) without any *if*'s, *and*'s or *but*'s. It is saying, like Abraham, "You are my God. My life is totally in your hands. Whatever you do, I will accept. What you say, I will believe. Whatever you command, I will do."

This is too clinical, by itself, like an X ray of a beautiful person. So *trust* must come, like a fire that comes to possess the iron pillar of decision. Trust says, "I will not only do what you say, I will be absolutely certain that it is *good* to do; I will trust you when my child is lying on the altar—or dead; I will not only believe what you say, I will *rest* in your words. Even in the darkest moment, when I may be hanging on some lonesome cross of pain or rejection and you ask me to hand over my spirit to you, I will let myself fall into the darkness, knowing you are there to catch me gently and hold me forever."

Happy Ending, New Beginning

Such is the faith of Abraham. Back at the mountain he is ready with the knife. He is on the point of becoming one of the tragic figures of history. He sets his jaw. Beneath the turbulence of horror and fear, faith and trust are the balance wheel.

Now the quick happy ending:

> But the LORD's messenger called to him from heaven. "Abraham, Abraham!"

A spasm of hope.

> "Do not lay your hand upon the boy," said the messenger. "Do not do the least thing to him. I know now how devoted you are to God, since you did not withhold from me your own beloved son." As Abraham looked about, he spied a ram caught by its horns in the thicket. So he went and took the ram and offered it up as a holocaust in place of his son. Abraham named the place Yahweh-yireh; hence people now say, "On the mountain the LORD will see." (Genesis 22:11a, 12-14)

Happy ending, like the Resurrection. We have seen many of them, and our faith should come easier for the knowledge. But the total gift of ourselves on an altar is still a fearful thing.

God didn't want Isaac, he wanted Abraham's total willingness, obedience and trust. His demand from us is the same, and our faith must stand at an altar without presuming the last-minute intervention of an angel. God's own heart was denied that luxury. He laid his own Son on the wood of Calvary, and held back the legions of angels who argued against the horror in God's own words to Abraham: "Your *Son*, your only one, whom you love!"

Abraham is our "father in faith" because he fulfilled the First Commandment: "I alone am God. You are receivers. Accept all I have to give you, for I love you, my children. But do not make a false god before me—your lust to be self-sufficient, independent, your daring even to seize the fruit of the tree. I will make you like God, like me, but do not try to *seize* that power, as the *adam* did."

On the mountaintop with Abraham the wounded world begins to feel God's healing. Abraham "succeeds" where our first parents failed and the world starts over with a promise, a covenant and a people. Humankind plunged from paradise to the pit of Babel. Now God begins the long climb upwards, carrying his people.

6.
The Plagues:
'Let My People Go!'

Suppose the government of the United States was afraid that
blacks were gaining too much power and took steps—cruel steps,
immoral steps—to grind them down. They must labor for a pittance on
public works projects, Congress decrees. When that doesn't break their
spirit, they are denied access to hospitals or medical help; many black
babies die.

Then suppose that one black mother, desperate to save her ailing
baby, lays the little form on the doorstep of the governor of Kentucky.
The governor's wife immediately calls the doctor and the baby is saved.
The governor's wife decides to adopt the baby, and asks a black maid
to take care of him—in the governor's mansion. The black woman just
happens to be the baby's mother.

No more problems for little Billy Ray. He gets a "white" name.
He is educated in the best of white schools and, after a brilliant
academic and athletic career at the University of Kentucky, he becomes

an administrative aide to a state senator.

But he never forgets his people. A deep anger seethes within him at their continued oppression. He feels guilty at the contrast between their life and his and is determined to build enough power in the white world to save them.

One day he attends a demonstration where blacks are demanding the right to Medicare and to decent working conditions. There is shouting and pushing, and police move in with dogs and clubs. He sees a young black man try to run past the police, only to be tripped up. Billy Ray sees the policeman's club rising and falling on the prostrate form. His anger overflows. A piece of pipe that was lying in the gutter is suddenly in his hand, and he flails wildly. The policeman slumps to the ground, dead. Billy Ray fades into the crowd. Knowing that he has been seen, he leaves the country. Billy Ray's story roughly parallels the early life of Moses as told in Exodus 1—30.

The stage was set for Moses' story when 70 Hebrew families, fleeing famine, came to Egypt. Four hundred years later they had grown to be a "nation within a nation" and the Egyptian pharaoh feared they could not be depended on in time of war. A time of enslavement and oppression began. They were put into forced labor, building the supply cities of Raamses and Pithom in the eastern part of the Nile Delta. But oppression only heightened their solidarity.

Pharaoh then commanded that every boy born to the Hebrews was to be thrown into the river. Moses' mother put him in the river herself—but in a papyrus basket waterproofed with pitch. As his sister watched, Pharaoh's daughter came to bathe. She found the baby and took him home, gave him an Egyptian name and raised him in the royal court.

Moses did not share his people's misery. In fact, he was probably embarrassed and guilty at the contrast. One day he saw an Egyptian foreman striking a Hebrew. He killed the Egyptian and hid his body in the sand. Afraid he would be exposed, he fled to Midian in the southern part of the Sinai Peninsula, where he remained for 10 years.

The Burning Bush

Now God, in order to forward his plan for the salvation of the world, opens Moses' eyes at the very mountain which would one day tremble as the same God made a covenant with his people and gave

them the Ten Commandments. From that event onward, the mountain will go down in history as Sinai (see Chapter 8), but here it is called Horeb—one clue that we are face to face with several biblical authors.

The author of the "burning bush" incident is known as "the Elohist" (E, in biblical shorthand) for his use of *Elohim* as the name of God. Reflecting a tradition which flourished in northern Israel about 950 B.C., the Elohist is more conscious of the distance between God and his creation than the Yawhist. Human encounters with God are much more formal than a walk in the garden; God speaks in dreams, in fire, in the voice of angels.

And so, an angel of the Lord (a phrase which can mean either God's messenger or God himself) appears to Moses as fire "flaming out of a bush" (Exodus 3:2*). Curious that the bush burns without being consumed, Moses goes closer to investigate the remarkable sight.

As Moses draws near, God has him remove his sandals:

> "...the place where you stand is holy ground....I am...the God of Abraham, the God of Isaac, the God of Jacob....I have witnessed the affliction of my people in Egypt and have heard their cry of complaint against their slave drivers, so I know well what they are suffering. Therefore I have come down to rescue them from the hands of the Egyptians and lead them out of that land into a good and spacious land, a land flowing with milk and honey....Come now! I will send you to Pharaoh to lead my people, the Israelites, out of Egypt."
>
> (3:5-8, 10)

Moses shrinks from the overwhelming task. Not only is he a fugitive, his own people have on occasion questioned his authority (see 2:14). But God says,

> *"I will be with you;* and this shall be your proof that it is I who have sent you: when you bring my people out of Egypt, you will worship God on this very mountain." (3:12, emphasis added)

Moses seems to recover his composure quickly. His curiosity rises. When the people ask him the name of the God who sent him, what should he say? He puts the question to God.

Among ancient Semitic peoples, to know someone's name is to

---

* Unless otherwise noted, Scripture citations in this chapter refer to the Book of Exodus.

have some measure of control over the other. (Remember the *adam* naming the animals back in Chapter 2.) But this God is beyond human control. He does not reveal his inner nature to Moses except to state that he is Being, necessary and absolute. God just *is,* and is the source of all life.

> God replied, "I am who am." Then he added, "This is what you shall tell the Israelites: I AM sent me to you." (3:14)*

God has taken another great step in his plan to liberate his people. Moses, later seen as a prototype of Jesus, has been appointed to lead his people from slavery to freedom—first from physical slavery, ultimately from the spiritual slavery of sin; first to political freedom, ultimately to the freedom of the children of God. We have come a long way from the creation story, which obviously had to be deduced and put into the Chosen People's own form of narrative. Now we are into *recorded* history—even though that history is seen and interpreted by faith.

Moses returns to Egypt with his brother, the priest Aaron. Together they go to ask Pharaoh to let the people go—just for a three-day journey into the desert to celebrate a feast in honor of their God.

"God, who?" is Pharaoh's response. To him the request is clearly a lazy people's strategy to avoid work. He is no fool, this Egyptian king; he adds more work. Moses, a true biblical man, complains to the Lord.

> "Lord, why do you treat these people so badly?"
> ...Then the LORD answered Moses: "Now you shall see what I will do to Pharaoh. Forced by my mighty hand, he will send them away....And now that I have heard the groaning of the Israelites, whom the Egyptians are treating as slaves, I am mindful of my covenant. I am the LORD. I will free you from the forced labor of the Egyptians and will deliver you from their slavery. I will rescue you

---

* "I am who am" is apparently the source of the word *Yahweh,* which the *New American Bible* translates as "LORD." Later Jewish religious custom held the name too sacred to be pronounced; *Adonai* ("Lord") took its place in speech. Since ancient Middle Eastern people used no vowels in writing, the proper pronunciation of the name (YHWH) was, in time, forgotten. In later history, the incorrect insertion of the vowels from *Adonai* coined the name *Yahoweh (Jehovah* in German).

by my outstretched arm and with mighty acts of judgment. I will take you as my own people, and you shall have me as your God."

(5:22; 6:1, 5-7)

The 10 Plagues

And so, God inflicts 10 plagues on the Egyptians—disasters of such intensity as to show his power. Here we again meet our old friends J and P in company with our new acquaintance, E. Some later editor has entwined their accounts of the plagues with great skill. J, the Yahwist who brings God close to his people, contributes eight of the plagues. For him, God intervenes directly at the word of Moses. The Elohist tells of five plagues, and his God is at work when Moses stretches forth his rod. Finally, the Priestly source recounts five plagues. This author understandably stresses the role of Aaron, the priest.

It is not at all unusual for even eyewitness accounts of a disaster to vary greatly in the details. Just so, the presence of these various traditions produces some varying viewpoints, even some contradictions. For instance, boils afflict "man and beast" in the sixth plague—yet "all the livestock of the Egyptians died" in the fifth (9:6, 10). One explanation is these two plagues are different authors' memories of the same event, as possibly the third and fourth plagues are also.

Again we remember: This is a *faith-book*. The point is that *God afflicted the Egyptians to save his people*. The details may vary, but the disaster (in this case the plagues) really happened. Once more we must remember that the biblical authors' first concern is God's doings. And God's doings, I mean to say, are more important than any human attempt to describe them.

God's immediate purpose is to force Pharaoh to let the Hebrews go worship in the desert. The ultimate purpose is

> "...so that the Egyptians may learn that I am the LORD as I stretch out my hand against Egypt and lead the Israelites out of their midst."

(7:5)

That is what the authors are preoccupied with. They see God acting. Whether these disasters could happen "naturally" would have seemed an idle question to them. We can't resist the question; we will consider "natural" explanations in a moment. But first, let's review what happened.

The First Plague (7:14-24; J, E, P): The water of the Nile turns to blood and becomes undrinkable. According to P and E, the change of water to blood makes it unfit to drink. For J the effect is less direct: The change in the water kills all the fish; their bodies pollute the water. The magicians of the Egyptian court duplicate the feat, and Pharaoh is unimpressed.

The Second Plague (7:25—8:11; J, P): At God's command, Moses has Aaron extend his staff over the streams. Frogs come out of the waters and infest the whole land. Once again, the Egyptian magicians produce the same effect. Nevertheless, Pharaoh promises to let the people go to offer sacrifice if Moses will pray that the plague be removed. When the request is granted, Pharaoh goes back on his word, but the first crack has appeared in his obstinancy. At each fresh blow he gives a little more.

The Third Plague (8:12-15; P): Aaron stretches out his staff and gnats—or mosquitoes—come up from the dry ground like a cloud of dust. Even the Egyptians could not do this. "This is the finger of God," they tell Pharaoh—but he does not yield.

The Fourth Plague (8:16-28; J): Flies swarm over the land—horseflies, perhaps, or dogflies—everywhere except the areas where the Israelites live. Pharaoh promises to allow the people to sacrifice—but not three days out into the desert. Moses insists it must be this far, for their sacrifices of cows, sheep, goats—sacred to the Egyptians—might spur the Egyptians to riot. Pharaoh agrees, the flies disappear. "Not one remained"—a greater wonder than their appearance in multitude. Again Pharaoh reneges on his word.

The Fifth Plague (9:1-7; J): Pestilence destroys all the livestock of the Egyptians. Though Pharaoh's messengers assure him that the Israelites' livestock have suffered no ill effect, he remains obdurate.

The Sixth Plague (9:8-12; P): At God's command, Moses and Aaron cast a double handful of soot into the sky. It turns to fine dust and afflicts every Egyptian it touches—human or animal—with painful boils. Now the magicians are not only powerless; they are themselves afflicted and cannot even stand in Moses' presence.

The Seventh Plague (9:13-35; J, E): The Elohist brings his awesome God onstage, and the drama begins to build. At his command, Moses stretches his hands toward heaven and brings down

> ...such fierce hail as had never been seen in the land....It struck down
> every man and beast that was in the open...;it splintered every tree in
> the fields. (9:24-25)

But in the Goshen area where the Israelites dwelt, no hail fell.

The Eighth Plague (10:1-20; J, E): Moses extends his hand over
the land and God's east wind brings a swarm of locusts into Egypt.

> They covered the surface of the whole land, till it was black with
> them....Nothing green was left on any tree or plant....(10:15)

Again the script: Pharaoh relents, a strong wind blows the locusts into
the sea, Pharaoh backtracks.

The Ninth Plague (10:21-29; J, E): Moses stretches his hand
toward the sky and a dense darkness—"such intense darkness that one
can feel it" (10:21)—comes over the land. It blankets Egypt for three
days—except where the Israelites dwell. This time Pharaoh promises to
let not only the men go, but the children as well. Only the Israelites'
flocks must remain behind. But Moses refuses his terms. How can his
people offer sacrifice if they have no herds from which to choose the
sacrificial animal? The angry Pharaoh orders Moses from his presence
once and for all.

The Tenth Plague (11:1-10; J, E, P): The final catastrophe is
announced. God will now perform his mightiest deed, striking down
every first-born in Egypt:

> "from the first-born of Pharaoh on the throne to the first-born of the
> slave-girl at the handmill, as well as all the first-born of the animals.
> Then there shall be loud wailing throughout the land of Egypt, such
> as has never been, nor will ever be again. But among the Israelites
> and their animals not even a dog shall growl...." (11:5-7)

The stage is set for the greatest moment in Israel's history: the
Exodus, which we will consider in the next chapter.

Natural or Supernatural?

The story of the plagues can be an insurmountable stumbling
block to the science-oriented mind and to those who have grown up
believing that God ordinarily acts through secondary causes—persons
or nature. Where do we draw the line between history and myth,

between natural event and miracle?

If you will, each of the 10 plagues can be explained "naturally"— at least up to a point.

1) As it swells before its annual flooding, the Nile picks up red deposits from the mountains of Africa and becomes the "Red Nile."

2) Frogs could have bred in the floodwaters of the Nile.

3) Mosquitoes are at their worst at the time of the Nile flooding, breeding in the drying, stagnant waters.

4) Ordinarily flies are in Egypt in such numbers as to be a pest (see Isaiah 7:18).

5) Cattle plagues are rare in Egypt, but severe when they do occur.

6) Diseases of the skin are common in Egypt. Here the connection between the dust and the boils may be based on skin irritation caused by a hot sirocco wind.

7) Hailstorms do sometimes occur.

8) Travelers today tell of clouds of locusts brought by the wind, then carried away as the wind changes.

9) The *khamsin,* a hot wind from the desert, carries an immense quantity of sand that darkens the atmosphere. Such sandstorms usually last three to four days.

10) The death of the first-born could have come from a deadly pestilence to which the Israelites were immune.

The question is, could the Israelite writers have lived in Egypt for four centuries without becoming aware of the frequent, even annual, occurrence of such phenomena? Hardly. Their point is that God *used* these things to show his power and to force Pharaoh to free them. They stress the unusual—miraculous—elements of the events: the suddenness with which pest and pestilence appeared and disappeared, the Egyptian magicians' inability to match Moses and Aaron, the fact that the Israelites were not affected, the intensity of the phenomena.

The writers of our faith-book wanted us to experience *God's power* protecting his people. Could they hear us ask *how* he did this, naturally or miraculously, they would not comprehend the question. God does *everything;* nothing is merely "natural."

It's like asking, "Did God act through my mother and father directly in showing me goodness and love, or was it all natural?" And when you've answered that question, there's another: Is there anything

43

in life that is merely "natural"?

I suspect this is a non-problem to most people, some of whom take the Bible as it stands, seeing God actually doing what the Bible says he's doing. On the other side are those who simply conclude that the whole story is just "imagination."

The second group is wrong on two counts. First, this *is* history here, no matter how "faith-ized." Second, they are unaware of the Semitic mind which saw God *directly* causing *everything—good and bad*. The biblical viewpoint is that if we win the war, God wins for us; if we lose the war, God is punishing us. If the tree bears fruit and grain sprouts from the ground, God is the actual cause; if the tree withers and the ground is sterile, God makes it so.

Our time has seen a drying up of the imagination and the wellsprings of poetry. We know God didn't cause the rainstorm; it was the fringe of a high pressure area in Iowa! God still gets blamed for "sending" crosses which he doesn't even explain: cancer, unfaithful spouses, unemployment, alcoholism; but as for color television, satellites, ice cream and computers, of course, *we* made them!

If we're going to read the Bible, we'll have to put on the biblical mind—and pray it stays on! We'll have to be aware how much science has dried up our awareness of the world outside the Massachusetts Institute of Technology. There is just one danger we need to avoid in the biblical viewpoint that God does all: Some innocent people may feel they *individually* are being punished in the sufferings that befall them.

If nuclear warheads destroy most of the population of Russia and the United States, the biblical mind would say that the *nations* are being punished—just as the *entire race* was lovingly cared for in every day's sunshine and rain, grain and fruit, family and friends. We are inextricably bound to each other. What one suffers, all suffer. That is the nature of human life. Only at the end will the wheat be separated from the chaff. God *could* stop all the bullets, dry up all evil thoughts, handcuff all criminals, erase all bad intentions—but then he would have a race of robots, not free people who must choose the path of their lives.

What it gets down to is this: God ordinarily lets the world of nature follow the laws he gave it. Ordinarily he does not stop human free will. He does not usually stop bullets or replace cancerous tissue or strike racists dead. At the same time, God must be behind everything;

the world would collapse into nothingness if he withdrew his creating/sustaining power. So we must say that God, in a sense, permits whatever happens in that world, since even the mind of a murderer would not "work" if God did not continue to keep him alive.

But God is not merely present as a sort of impersonal energy. He is present like an eager guest, at the center of every mind, hoping his light will turn that person to truth. He is present, like an ardent lover, at the threshold of every human heart at every moment of the day, hoping that his own love will enter the strivings of that heart. And sometimes God breaks into his creation by direct intervention. He certainly did this in Jesus and in the early Church's experiences of the risen Christ. He certainly does it in the sacramental actions of the Church.

And he certainly did it for his Chosen People in the stories we are about to consider: in the Exodus, in the capture of the Promised Land, in all that was necessary to further his plan to save the world in Jesus.

7.

Exodus:
Mud Road to Glory

The world can never be the same after that first atomic bomb sent its deadly mushroom cloud over the New Mexico desert. For all time, that picture will be a symbol of what can only be called humankind's death wish. No words need to be spoken—just at the sight of the picture our hearts will shrink a little. The *symbol* is powerful. It "realizes" reality.

The most powerful symbol in the New Testament is the cross. It captures the central reality of all time—the death and resurrection of Jesus. True, we can get used to it, as we grow accustomed to many sacred symbols—wedding rings, the flag, bread and wine. But when the chips are down, when the doctor starts to mumble generalities, we want the cross between our fingers with the beads we may not have used for years.

The cross of Good Friday and the sunrise of Easter Sunday combine to form the symbol of *the* Great Exodus—Jesus' triumphant and liberating passage through death to a new life that can never be lost. His passage—now a passageway—is open to us. We can go through his death to life in Baptism. Nothing in life or death has more meaning to a Christian than the death and resurrection of Jesus.

Now, if Christians want to understand the faith of Jews—and the roots of their own—they must realize that what the death and resurrection of Jesus is to them, the Exodus, the deliverance from slavery in Egypt, is to the Jews. For them this story is the heart of the Bible, *the* symbol of God's love and saving grace, the center of time. Together with the covenant at Sinai, it is the explanation of all their life, the bedrock of a faith that has been tested in pain and persecution for 30 centuries.

So important is the story they told it over and over again. The Book of Exodus contains three accounts of the event. The oldest was written somewhere between the 12th and 11th century B.C. (The Exodus itself took place in the 13th century B.C.) This oldest account is found in Exodus 15:1-12; it is a hymn, the triumphant song of Moses and the people of Israel after the successful escape.

A second account is from the Priestly source. A third is from both the Yahwist and Elohist traditions, put together in the eighth century B.C. These two versions are intertwined in the 31 verses of Exodus 14.

I mention these dull facts to emphasize another fact: The Bible accounts we are reading are, unlike the creation accounts, memories of actual events in Jewish history. Further, these events were deeply meditated on by a people with faith in God and therefore seen as having far deeper meaning than the mere facts would indicate. In fact, the Exodus account seems at least in part to have been taken from recitations used in the liturgy over many centuries. (As many scholars suspect, a similar phenomenon occurs in the New Testament: The Church didn't look into the New Testament to find out how to have Eucharist; rather, when the Church wrote the New Testament, it simply included the liturgical texts of the Eucharist that had already been celebrated over several decades.)

The Historical Event

The Exodus was not a very dramatic happening—just a footnote in the history of Egypt. Like Jesus' crucifixion hidden away outside the walls of Jerusalem, it may have seemed almost an anticlimax.

It began during the terrible night of the 10th plague, at the deaths of the Egyptian first-born. Pharaoh summoned Moses and Aaron and told them to leave at once, with all their people. The Egyptian people, fearing they would die too, urged them to do the same, even donating clothing and silver and gold objects. Note that what Pharaoh was permitting was that they could "go worship the LORD as you said" (Exodus 12:31*)—presumably a three-day journey into the desert *and back*.

The Israelites, in a hurry, baked their dough without waiting for it to rise and wrapped their kneading bowls in their cloaks (see 12:39). Hence the use of unleavened bread in the later liturgical remembrance: "the bread of affliction, that you may remember as long as you live the day of of your departure from the land of Egypt; for in frightened haste you left the land of Egypt" (Deuteronomy 16:3).

How many people left Egypt? Scholars estimate the number as being several thousand—taking the "six hundred thousand men on foot, not counting the children" of 12:37 as a "Semitic exaggeration."

The route? The Bible itself excludes the easy shoreline road. Also excluded are two other routes that would have been well-traveled and patrolled by government troops. So the actual course is a matter of speculation. One is reminded of the Underground Railroad whereby abolitionists rescued many slaves before the Civil War. There was no one precise route. So here: It didn't matter how they went; what is important to the authors is God's liberating operation.

At any rate, Pharaoh seems suddenly to have realized that the Israelites hadn't merely gone a three-days' journey into the desert to worship. *They weren't coming back,* and he was losing a gigantic free labor pool. He mustered his charioteers and went into hot pursuit. His soldiers caught up with Moses and his little band of fugitives at the edge of a body of water.

The *New American Bible* keeps the term *Red Sea* while the *Jerusalem Bible* says *the Sea of Reeds*. The Hebrew word actually means "Reed Sea" and may refer to a body of water that ancient texts call the "Papyrus Marsh." Some locate it south of the Bitter Lakes in Egypt. On the other hand, at the time of the Exodus (the topography has since changed) these lakes were somehow connected with the tip of

---

* Unless otherwise noted, Scripture citations in this chapter refer to the Book of Exodus.

the long arm of the Red Sea that penetrates between Egypt and the Sinai.

Wherever it was, the fugitives stood at the edge of the water, watching Pharaoh's troops closing in on them. They vented their fear on poor Moses, as they would later in the desert. Weren't there any burial places in Egypt, that he had to bring them out into the desert to die? They even advanced a "better Red than dead" argument: "Far better for us to be slaves of the Egyptians than to die in the desert" (14:12).

A patient God held his temper and told Moses to lift his staff and stretch out his hand to "split the sea in two, that the Israelites may pass through it on dry land" (14:16). As Cecil B. DeMille eagerly read, the sea did split and became "like a wall to their right and to their left" (14:22). They marched through. When the Egyptians tried to follow, their chariot wheels became so clogged that they could hardly move. Moses applied the coup de grace when he stretched out his hand and the waters flowed back, drowning every single Egyptian.

The actual crossing was probably much less dramatic. Some scholars would say we simply don't know what happened. Others attempt explanation. *The New Catholic Commentary on Holy Scripture* has this to say:

> At the time of the exodus this sea [the Red Sea] communicated with the Bitter Lakes from which it was separated by a shallow bank of sand and extensive marshes. A ford, which the Israelites intended to cross, provided a passage across the marshes. The use of the ford much depended on the flow of the waters, which were tidal and influenced by the elements. *By God's providential act* the marshes were fordable at the right time for the Israelites, while the Egyptians could not avail themselves of this opportunity.
>
> (p.214, emphasis added).

The View of Faith

Remember, again, that when the Book of Exodus was written, many centuries had passed and the Jews had had time to reflect on the presence of God's hand guiding their history. Their liturgy, as we have said, incorporated these accounts of God's saving actions. Their faith, it cannot be said too often, simply saw God doing everything—sending rain and shine, pain and pleasure, victory and defeat. So, whatever happened, God did it.

Since God did it, it was glorious. If it was glorious, it should be described with majesty. Hence we may easily get the impression that the Israelite people moved out of Egypt like a mile-wide phalanx of Patton tanks, with the massive precision of a Moscow May Day parade. Actually, they may have straggled out over a period of time, a motley and ragged string of escapees, hardly knowing what was happening, looking back over their shoulders. No matter. With faith, later, they saw that God was leading them.

Scholars have pointed out that Cecil B. DeMille's movie portrayal of the water standing in perfect perpendicular suspense is too literal a reading of the Bible, which itself says that God "swept the sea with a strong east wind throughout the night and so turned it into dry land" (14:12). The writers saw no incongruity in adding immediately that the water was like a wall, just as the song of Moses speaks of God's breath piling up the waters so that they "stood like a mound" (13:8).

It cannot be said too often: the Bible gives us *interpreted events*. Bible writers made no fetish of "objective" reporting, video-taped and cassette-recorded accounts. But our vaunted network news is no less interpretive by the very fact that it is selective.

If Dan Rather opens the news with the account of a Jewish-Arab confrontation instead of a Sino-Russian border incident, he is making a value judgment, a subjective interpretation that one story is more important than the other. He also makes a subjective judgment that it is not important, on any given night, to mention the number of abortions that day, the number of people who entered contemplative orders or the number of children who starved to death.

Similarly the reporter, who "objectively" notes the exact spot where the dead body lay and what the people said, does not ordinarily ask whether or not the man prayed before he died. Nor does another journalist, who carefully reports the race of the suspect in a robbery, tell readers whether his mother loved him or not.

So, if we allow Frank Reynolds to make his subjective value judgment as to what is important news, we should also let Bible writers view things from what they held to be the central fact of life: their relationship to God. The biblical authors recorded the *faith* of the Jewish nation in the God who actually saved them.

Thus, the fact that there was once a captive people in Egypt and some years later that same people was free in the Promised Land meant only one thing: *God saved them*. The Exodus now becomes the primary symbol of God's relationship with humankind: Savior.

It doesn't matter, then, whether the Israelites came out of Egypt like Sherman going through Georgia, or like thousands of black slaves straggling north through the Underground Railroad. God brought them out.

Passover

Down through the centuries even to our day, Jews have kept the Exodus event alive in the annual celebration of Passover. So closely related are the event and the feast that the Bible leaves the Israelites standing, bags packed and ready to leave Egypt, while the regulations for Passover and the consecration of the first-born are spelled out in a long passage (12:43—13:17).

The meaning of the word *passover—pesah* in Hebrew—is difficult to establish. In popular biblical terms, it is connected with the verb "to jump." Yahweh "jumped"—passed over—the houses of the Hebrews.

Scholars find great similarity between the biblical Passover rite and a pagan rite of ancient nomadic Arabs, and it should be no surprise if the early Jews did in fact make that rite their own (as Christians later took over the December Feast of Rising Sun and made it Christmas). They too were shepherds, semi-nomadic.

Originally, these shepherds sacrificed a young animal to obtain fertility for the whole flock and put the animal's blood on the tent poles to drive away evil spirits. Signs of a nomadic people are seen in the fact that the victim was roasted (not boiled or raw), cooked in the manner of people on the march; that the meat was eaten with unleavened bread (there was no time to wait for yeast dough to rise), and bitter herbs (i.e., wild, uncultivated). The participants were to be dressed for immediate departure, with shepherd crooks in hands. (Those who have read James Michener's *The Caravans* will remember the picture of the desolate landscape of Afghanistan and the nomadic Kochis breaking camp to seek warmer climates and green pastures, traveling in the brillance of a full moon.)

Two things should be noted about the Passover account in Exodus. First, according to Bible scholars, it represents an "historicizing" of earlier celebrations. This unmanageable word simply means that, as the centuries went by, more and more new saving acts of God were telescoped into one and celebrated by the Passover rite. A faintly similar example might be our Veteran's Day, which added the memorializing of WWII to that of Armistice Day of WWI.

Second, the account in Exodus 12 also reflects *later* practices in Israel: not just what happened at first, but the liturgy as it had developed centuries later. (Remember that Exodus took place around 1250 B.C.; the Old Testament was not put into writing until hundreds of years later.)

But in all our discussions and reading, let the central fact never be missed: God did it. God brought his people out of Egypt by his mighty hand. He liberated them from slavery and brought them through water to freedom. If we have time, we may want to study *how*. We may even find some human answers like east winds drying up causeways and then turning them back into marshes. All very interesting, even important, but secondary.

In the Exodus, God established for all history a metaphor which would be fulfilled perfectly in Jesus as he strode valiantly into the darkness of death and thereby into the glory of freedom and eternal life. He is the first-born who turned the old story around. His own blood on the wood saved not only the first-born of his people, but the whole world.

8.
'I Love You and I'll Marry You, My Cantankerous People!'

So now the slave is off the plantation, brought up through the Underground Railroad and dumped onto a country lane in Indiana. What next? Well, it is a long trek through the boondocks before there is a nice home in suburban Detroit and a good job at the Ford plant. And sometimes it will seem that the old plantation wasn't so bad after all.

God didn't, however, just dump his people into a desert without resources; but he didn't whisk them to the Promised Land on a magic carpet, either. He gave them his promise, and he gave them Moses. They would have to trust and wait. It would be a long time before they crossed the Jordan into the Promised Land—40 years, the Bible says. Mathematical exactness is not the point here; *40 years* can mean "a full generation" or, more vaguely, "a long time." But it is approximately correct: None of the adults who left Egypt got to enter the Promised Land; a new generation, under the leadership of Joshua, had that privilege (cf. *Understanding the Old Testament,* by B.W. Anderson).

Whatever the time frame, the journey through the desert was a time of stormy courtship with their loving Yahweh. They were hardly across the miraculous water and barely acquainted with the rigors of desert life when they began to long for the fleshpots of Egypt. They could taste the garlic.

First they grumbled because they had no water for three days—and when they finally found some at Marah, it was bitter. God showed Moses a certain kind of wood which, when thrown into the water, made it fresh.

In a few more months the Israelites grumbled against Moses as they wandered in the Sinai desert:

> "Would that we had died at the LORD's hand in the land of Egypt, as we sat by our fleshpots and ate our fill of bread! But you had to lead us into this desert to make the whole community die of famine!"
>
> (Exodus 16:3*)

God sighed, and gave them manna and quail.

Next they quarreled with Moses because of water—again. So God told Moses,

> "Go over there in front of the people, along with some of the elders of Israel, holding in your hand, as you go, the staff with which you struck the river. I will be standing there in front of you on the rock of Horeb. Strike the rock, and the water will flow from it for the people to drink." (17:5)

The water came, of course.

You have to give it to the Israelites. At least they were honest about their sins. They named the place *Massah* and *Meribah*—"the place of the test" and "the place of quarreling"—because they had "quarreled there and tested the Lord, saying, 'Is the Lord in our midst or not?'" (17:7).

The Book of Numbers recounts still another water incident when Moses struck the rock—for water, as God told him to—but *twice*, perhaps in anger, or because he began to doubt God's power and felt he had to open the spring himself.

We telescope time now—40 years or so. We come to the

---

* Unless otherwise noted, Scripture citations in this chapter refer to the Book of Exodus.

56

Mountain of the Covenant—the second act of the Exodus drama, the formalizing of God's marriage to his people. The mountain is Sinai (Horeb), a massive altar of granite somewhere in the Sinai peninsula (its exact location has been lost to memory).

Something big is in the air. God tells Moses to have the people consecrate themselves for two days, to wash their garments and be ready for the third day. When the trumpet sounds, they are to come to the mountain.

> On the morning of the third day there were peals of thunder and lightning, and a heavy cloud over the mountain, and a very loud trumpet blast, so that all the people in the camp trembled. But Moses led the people out of the camp to meet God, and they stationed themselves at the foot of the mountain. Mount Sinai was all wrapped in smoke, for the LORD came down upon it in fire. The smoke rose from it as though from a furnace, and the whole mountain trembled violently. The trumpet blast grew louder and louder, while Moses was speaking and God answering him with thunder. (19:16-19)

It was thrilling (to scientists) and awesome (to believers): Moses daring to speak to God under the heavy clouds while the wind rushed over the mountain peaks and over the trembling crowd. Lightning revealed the harsh outline of the Sinai, then the magnificent skywide rumbling thunder, rolling through the valleys like a flood, boomed like the shock of a thousand cannons.

It was God's trumpet, God's face quickly flashing and then invisible again. It was God's voice softened into rumbling echoes, dying away in the desert, then shaking the mountaintop again.

Just another storm? Yes, the way Alamogordo was just another bomb, as the Red Sea was just another barefoot walk across a muddy causeway.

Was it a volcano? Not necessarily. Thunder and lightning and wind and darkness will do.

But most important is what God *meant* by the display and what Jewish and Christian faith *learned* from the cosmic fireworks. "Tell the Israelites," God said to Moses:

> "You have seen for yourselves how I treated the Egyptians and how I bore you up on eagle wings and brought you here to myself. Therefore, if you hearken to my voice and keep my covenant, you shall be my special possession, dearer to me than all other people,

57

though all the earth is mine. You shall be to me a kingdom of priests, a holy nation! That is what you must tell the Israelites." So Moses went and summoned the elders of the people. When he set before them all that the LORD had ordered him to tell them, the people all answered together, "Everything the LORD has said, we will do." Then Moses brought back to the LORD the response of the people. (19:4-8)

Covenant

This exchange of promises, the covenant, stands with the Exodus as the foundation rock of Old Testament faith. It is the final flowering of Exodus, God taking his people to himself in marriage. Because so much is involved, we will have to spend some time getting the background.

The word *covenant* means, literally, "a coming together." In a culture without written records, it was a verbal agreement solemnly made before witnesses, with sacrifical rites and the acceptance of a curse in case of nonfulfillment (recall the covenant ceremony with Abraham, pp. 29-30).

Covenants could be made between equals, but obviously God and Israel are not equal. Their covenant more closely resembles a historical phenomenon called by the odd name of *suzerainty:* a sovereign's covenant, one imposed by an overlord.

"Overlord" is not an appealing name for God, but of course he *is* absolute Lord over all. Only Yahweh could promise the kind of future which was revealed to Abraham. Only God could *choose* a people peculiarly his own, and only God could offer the kind of covenant the Jews received:

> For love of your fathers he chose their descendants and personally led you out of Egypt by his great power. (Deuteronomy 4:37)

Israel realized their unique privilege:

> "For what great nation is there that has gods so close to it as the LORD our God is to us whenever we call upon him?" (Deuteronomy 4:7)

But the covenant was a call for responsibility and maturity as well as gift and privilege. They had to recognize reality—Yahweh is the only God—and keep his commandments.

Still, the covenant was a source of blessing as well as obligation. True, the blessing was dependent upon observance. God, the suzerain, was not unfaithful if he punished his people for violating the covenant.

But we are already becoming too legalistic. The simplest expression of the covenant echoes marriage vows: "...I will be your God and you shall be my people" (Jeremiah 7:23; see also Jeremiah 11:4; 24:7; Ezekiel 11:20; 14:11; Hosea 2:25). It *was* a marriage—the marriage of a truly loving, trusting, faithful God to a bridal people that was not particularly attractive, but desired; not beautiful or even virtuous, but loved as the apple of God's eye.

Israel was an *adulterous* people—the description crops up often in the Old Testament—but one whom a forgiving husband always took back. The prophet Hosea, playing the character of God, did what no self-respecting Jewish husband would do: took back his three-time adulterous wife, Gomer (see Hosea 1—3).

There is a word that the Bible uses for this special love God gives: *hesed*. Scholars say it is hard to translate. It means kinship love, kindness beyond the call of duty, the love of the tenderest husband for his bride. It is forgiving and unquenchable, a fiery and passionate love. It is often translated awkwardly, "steadfast covenant love." Awkward, indeed, but rugged. It kept a stormy marriage alive.

The Psalmist expresses this love:

> I will punish their offenses with the rod,
> Then I will scourge them on account of their guilt.
> But I will never take back my love:
> My truth will never fail.
> I will never violate my covenant
> Nor go back on the word I have spoken.
> (Psalm 89: 31-34, Grail translation)

Israel's part in the covenant is found in the Law. After the ecstatic moment of Sinai the Israelites received, through Moses, the Book of the Covenant. It begins with Exodus 21—pages and pages of laws. (Those who insist that everything in the Bible has equal value and that one must do "whatever the Bible says," allowing no place for moral development or change in nonessentials, will find great difficulty if they include Exodus 21—23 and 25—30 and the whole Book of Leviticus in their reading!) The Israelites did not think of these laws as oppressive or confining. They were ways of keeping the covenant, of maintaining the kind of peoplehood that the covenant required.

But placed before this Book of the Covenant—or, rather, forming its preface—are the "Ten Words" (the literal meaning of *Decalogue*), which we call the Ten Commandments (20:1-17). They are not themselves a *code* of law; they are not concerned with details. Rather, they are a summing up, a setting forth of the purpose of all law.

Through these "Ten Words" God tells his people how they can fulfill their "side" of the Covenant. They are a way of expressing grateful love in response to the steadfast covenant love Yahweh promises them.

In the later light of Jesus' new commandment of love, the last six commandments—the negative ones—seem minimalistic. They are "merely" what any thinking human being should ultimately conclude after surveying the nature of human society. They are primitive, in the sense that they were given to a people who had not yet developed a fine sense of morality. (That would come later, under the gentle and stormy urgings of the prophets.)

There they are, negative and primitive if you will, but still essential building blocks of morality. Unlike the pagans around them, the Israelites did not have to worry about placating a gaggle of gods who were as unstable as themselves; they were not, at least in principle, obsessed by demons or magic. They had one personal God, Yahweh, the steadfast covenant-lover, and they were his people.

Faithless People, Faithful God

The exact sequence of events after the giving of the Commandments is not clear. But two things evidently did happen.

First, Moses presided at a "way-out" liturgy. He announced the ordinances of the Lord to the people, and they answered with one voice, promising to do everything that the Lord commanded. Pure wedding-day resolve.

Young bulls were sacrificed as peace offerings. Moses took half of the blood and splashed it on the altar. Then he read the Book of the Covenant to the people and they said again:

"All that the LORD has said, we will heed and do." (24:7)

Moses took the remaining blood and sprinkled it on the people, saying,

> "This is the blood of the covenant which the LORD has made with you in accordance with all these words of his." (24:8)

Blood is life, much more sacred to these Jews than to us today. Blood on the altar, blood on the people: one life in God and in his people.

Moses went back up the mountain and stayed there for 40 days. It got long for the people below. Amazingly fickle, they besought a weak Aaron.

> "Come, make us a god who will be our leader; as for the man Moses who brought us out of the land of Egypt, we do not know what has happened to him." (32:1)

Aaron collected their jewelry and fashioned a golden idol. It was probably a bull (although the author disdainfully calls it a calf). The Israelites would have been familiar with the bull-gods—Baal of the Canaanites and Apis of the Egyptians. Quickly forgetting the first of Yahweh's commands,

> ...they cried out, "This is your God, O Israel, who brought you out of the land of Egypt." (32:4)

Up on the mountain, God was incensed and told Moses that his anger would blaze against his people and consume them.

> "Then I will make of you [Moses] a great nation." (32:10)

Moses prayed for his people, and the Lord relented. But when Moses came down from the mountain, carrying the two stone tablets inscribed with the Ten Commandments, he saw the pagan revelry of the people. Losing his temper, he smashed the tablets at the base of the mountain.

But God's mercy triumphed. He had Moses cut two new tablets and called him back up the mountain. There God described himself to Moses:

> The LORD, the LORD, a merciful and gracious God, slow to anger and rich in kindness and fidelity, continuing his kindness for a thousand generations, and forgiving wickedness and crime and sin; yet not declaring the guilty guiltless but punishing children and grandchildren to the third and fourth generations for their fathers' wickedness!
>
> (34:6-7)

Then God renewed the covenant:

> "Here, then,...is the covenant I will make. Before the eyes of all your people I will work such marvels as have never been wrought in any nation anywhere on earth, so that this people among whom you live may see how awe-inspiring are the deeds which I, the LORD, will do at your side. But you, on your part, must keep the commandments I am giving you today." (34:10-11)

The pattern is set. The love affair between God and his people will continue as it began—a dreary cycle of sin and punishment, from one viewpoint; an endless stream of God's forgiveness and faithfulness, from another.

9.
David the Adulterer: Penitent King After God's Own Heart

Sinners can take heart from David's history. Thanks to Hollywood's efforts, many of us know only one thing about him: his adultery with Bathsheba and his ordering the murder of her husband. Yet he is Israel's greatest king, seen by Christians as a prototype of Jesus, and the author of some of the prayers that are still said all over the world every day—the Psalms.

We have telescoped time here. We left the Israelites in the desert where they wandered for a generation before entering Canaan—the land to which God called Abraham centuries earlier—and settling into farming its valleys. For a century and a half they remained a loose confederation of 12 tribes who looked to a series of judges for leadership. Early in the 11th century B.C. a growing threat from the Philistines united them in defense of their land.

Their new awareness of themselves as a nation led to an outcry for a king to govern them. The elders of the tribes went to the prophet

Samuel and asked him to appoint a king "as other nations have"
(1 Samuel 8:5). Samuel talked it over with God, who was reluctant—
God thought *he* was the king of Israel. God sent Samuel back to the
people with a lecture on the evils of a monarch:

> "He will take your sons and assign them to his horses and
> chariots....He will use your daughters as ointment-makers, as cooks,
> and as bakers....He will tithe your crops and your vineyards....He
> will take your male and female servants....He will tithe your flocks
> and you yourselves will become his slaves." (1 Samuel 8:11, 13-17)

But the elders would not be talked out of the idea. God sighed,
and gave them their king: Saul, whose military prowess was offset by a
choleric personality.

The Lord soon regretted his choice. He sent Samuel to the home
of Jesse in Bethlehem, "for I have chosen my king from among his
sons." Seven of these stalwarts passed in review before the prophet,
and all were rejected. "Is that all?" "Oh yes, there's David out there
with the sheep, but surely—" They sent for the boy. He was "ruddy, a
youth handsome to behold and making a splendid appearance"
(1 Samuel 16:12). Unbeknown to Saul, Samuel anointed David, and
"the Spirit of the LORD rushed upon David" (1 Samuel 16:13).

Saul's Jealousy

Poor, tormented Saul wanted someone to play the harp before
him when he was in one of his fits of melancholy. He sent for David at
the advice of a servant who said David was "a stalwart soldier, besides
being an able speaker, and handsome. Moreover, the LORD is with him"
(1 Samuel 16:18). So David came into Saul's service—and
immediately entered into a deep friendship with Jonathan, the king's
son. Somehow Saul's neurotic mind conceived a ridiculous suspicion
that David would endanger the succession of Jonathan.

There were other reasons why Saul felt threatened. David was
popular, and he was brave. In one of the endless wars with their
perennial enemies the Philistines, the Israelites faced a champion six
and a half feet tall. Goliath was the "mean Joe Green" of his day. His
spearhead alone weighed 15 pounds and his armor 125, give or take
some editorial license. He taunted the Israelites: "I defy the ranks of
Israel today. Give me a man and let us fight together" (1 Samuel

17:10)—winner take all. David volunteered and was promptly rejected by Saul: "You're just a youth!" But David argued that as a shepherd he had killed lions and bears, and the same Lord who had protected him then would keep him safe now. Saul dressed the boy in his own armor and sent him out to battle.

David could hardly walk with Saul's armor, so he shucked that. He chose five smooth stones from the bed of a stream and approached the giant with only a sling. The champion was insulted, of course. A handsome teenager sent against the terror of the battlefield, a pretty youth against John Wayne! But David answered his insults with a declaration of faith:

> "You come against me with sword and spear and scimitar, but I come against you in the name of the LORD of hosts, the God of the armies of Israel that you have insulted." (1 Samuel 17:45)

David will kill Goliath, and "the whole land shall learn that Israel has a God" (1 Samuel 17:46).

They met at close quarters. David took a stone and hurled it with his sling. It embedded itself in Goliath's forehead and the giant fell to the ground. David took the Philistine's own sword and cut off his head.

Israel had won a round of the endless war, but now Saul had a new worry. The women sang,

> "Saul has slain his thousands,
>   and David his ten thousands." (1 Samuel 18:7)

Like Macbeth speaking of Banquo, Saul began to mutter. "All that's left for him is the kingship."

The next day, when Saul was in one of his rages, David came to play for him. Suddenly Saul hurled his spear at the singer—twice, apparently—hoping to nail him to the wall, but David escaped.

Saul got David out of his presence by making him a leader of Israel's armies. Surely the upstart would die on the battlefield! The ploy failed, and David grew in popularity with his continued success as a military leader.

David the Fugitive

Saul's rage and envy finally made it necessary for David to take to the desert, a refugee. Around him gathered "all those who were in

difficulties or in debt, or who were embittered" (1 Samuel 22:2). Four hundred of these unlikely warriors made him their leader. Ultimately, Saul decided to pursue David into the desert, and a choice story resulted. Saul paused in his pursuit and entered a cave occupied by David and his men. Hiding in its inner recesses, David's followers were delighted: The Lord had delivered David's enemy into his grasp!

But David moved up silently only to cut off a piece of Saul's mantle, telling his men, "The LORD forbid that I should...lay a hand on him, for he is the LORD's anointed" (1 Samuel 24:7). Saul left the cave, oblivious to what had happened. When he had gone a safe distance, David emerged, waving the scrap of fabric, and called to him:

> "Why do you listen to those who say, 'David is trying to harm you'? You see for yourself today that the LORD just now delivered you into my grasp in the cave....[But] I will take no action against you....Whom are you pursuing? A dead dog, or a single flea?"
>
> (1 Samuel 24:10-11, 14-15)

Saul wept aloud with anger, relief and shame. "May the LORD reward you generously for what you have done this day!" (1 Samuel 24:20). He admitted that David would surely be king, and asked only that his own descendants be not destroyed!

Saul's remorse was short-lived, and he soon resumed the pursuit. Once more David spared the king's life: This time, at night, David and his men came upon Saul sleeping and took the spear that lay beside his head.

Saul died by his own hand after seeing his sons slain and being wounded himself in battle with the Philistines at Mt. Gilboa (see 1 Samuel 31:1-6). Though he was a tragic figure, one with whom the Lord no longer walked, he was the first anointed king of Israel. David expressed his own and the nation's grief in a famous dirge:

> "Alas! the glory of Israel, Saul,
>   slain upon your heights;
> how can the warriors have fallen!
>
> "Tell it not in Gath,
>   herald it not in the streets of Ashkelon,
> Lest the Philistine maidens rejoice,
>   lest the daughters of the strangers exult!
> Mountains of Gilboa,
>   may there be neither dew nor rain upon you,

nor upsurgings of the deeps!
Upon you lie begrimed the warriors' shields,
    the shield of Saul, no longer anointed with oil....

"Saul and Jonathan, beloved and cherished,
separated neither in life nor in death,
    swifter than eagles, stronger than lions!

..."I grieve for you, Jonathan my brother!
    most dear have you been to me;
More precious have I held love for you
    than love for women.

"How can the warriors have fallen,
    the weapons of war have perished!"

(2 Samuel 1:19-21, 23, 25-27)

David the King

About the year 1000 B.C. David was anointed king at Hebron (at
present one of the cities in the famous West Bank area)—but king of
just one tribe, Judah. The other 11 tribes followed Saul's general Abner
and recognized Saul's son Ish-Baal as king. The ensuing civil war
ended with the assassination (against David's will) of both these men,
and David was made king of all 12 tribes. He made Jerusalem his royal
city, and brought the Ark of the Covenant, containing the stone tablets
on which Moses had inscribed the Commandments, there. He would
have built a temple if he had not been deterred by a divine oracle.
Through the prophet Nathan, God politely declined David's offer to
build him a house. Generously, God turned the tables: He promised to
establish a house for David and his descendants—a house that will
endure:

> "Your house and your kingdom shall endure forever before me; your
> throne shall stand firm forever." (2 Samuel 7:16)

This was the promise which gave hope to Israel when their
fortunes failed; for among the descendants of David, the Jews believed,
would come a new king, the Messiah. (Christians still honor as King
one who could trace his ancestry to David: Jesus of Nazareth.)

It seems an ideal picture: a great king secured on his throne by
God himself, Israel united under him. But David had constantly to
contend with revolts within his country, with attacks from surrounding
nations—and with his own sinfulness.

68

David the Sinner

Hollywood had a made-to-order sequence in the dark cloud that hung over David's life. (Less attention is paid to his great repentance; many of the Psalms are probably the cry of a great and sensitive soul who realizes the depth of his sin.) He committed adultery with Bathsheba, the beautiful wife of Uriah the Hittite. When Bathsheba became pregnant, David tried to cover his deed by sending Uriah off to the front line, ordering his officers to pull back and leave Uriah to die at the enemy's hands. The plan worked, and David took the lovely widow home as his bride.

The great drama lies in the way Nathan the prophet trapped David into repentance. He came to the king with a story:

> "Judge this case for me! In a certain town there were two men, one rich, the other poor. The rich man had flocks and herds in great numbers. But the poor man had nothing at all except one little ewe lamb that he had bought. He nourished her, and she grew up with him and his children. She shared the little food he had and drank from his cup and slept in his bosom. She was like a daughter to him. Now, the rich man received a visitor, but he would not take from his own flocks and herds to prepare a meal for the wayfarer who had come to him. Instead he took the poor man's ewe lamb and made a meal of it for his visitor." (2 Samuel 12:1-4)

David's response was ferocious. His sensitive soul was outraged at the injustice. He exploded:

> "As the LORD lives, the man who has done this merits death! He shall restore the ewe lamb fourfold because he has done this and has had no pity." (2 Samuel 12:5-6)

Then Nathan quietly sprang the trap door. He let David's words bounce around the walls until the echo died. He let a long silence hang in the air. Then he dared to fix his eyes on the king and say, very softly: *"You are the man!"* (2 Samuel 12:7).

David was crushed, caught in his own condemnation. But he had the grace to be honest. "I have sinned," he admitted.

Thus did Jesus acquire an ancestor who was not only a great king, a sensitive poet, a symbol of all that was best in Israel. He was also an adulterer, a murderer—and a penitent.

The Bible calls David a man after God's own heart. That's quite a consolation for the rest of us, who are burdened with the ancient heresy that if we do not manage perfect lives by our own strength, God will have nothing to do with us. David was a man of blood and lust. But he was also one who had sense enough to accept God's punishment and healing. And so we are back to the theme that emerges through the pages of the Old Testament: The fundamental fact of life is our total dependence on God; the fundamental sin is arrogant self-sufficiency; the fundamental nature of God is love, mercy, forgiveness.

10.
Ruth the Serene

There are places in the world where a journey of no more than 25 or 30 miles means being faced with a new language and a new culture—a trip through the Brenner Pass from Germany to Italy, for instance. One of the loveliest women in the Bible took such a journey and embraced a wholly new life simply because she loved her mother-in-law.

The story begins with a famine in Bethlehem. A man named Elimelech took his wife Naomi and their two sons and went through Jerusalem down the desert road to Jericho—probably the same route Jesus spoke of in his story of the man who fell among robbers. It is dry, hot desert all the way. They crossed the Jordan near the Dead Sea and went through the towering mountains that press against the eastern shore of the oily sea into the land of Moab. There they settled.

Three deaths left three widows. Naomi's husband died first; then some years later both her sons, who had married Moabite (pagan) women, Orpha and Ruth. Sad and homesick, Naomi heard that back home in Bethlehem the drought had ended. Or, in the Biblical view, "the LORD had visited his people and given them food" (Ruth 1:6*).

She began the hot journey home, and it seemed natural for her two daughters-in-law to go with her. But on the way she realized what it would do to them. Naomi knew the emotional cost of living in an alien culture, even with a husband and children. She could not allow these Moabite women, now widows, to leave their native land. She stopped and said to them:

> "Go back, each of you...May the LORD be kind to you as you were to the departed and to me! May the LORD grant each of you a husband and a home in which you will find rest." (1:8-9).

She kissed them good-by, but they wept loudly and insisted they would return with her to her people.

Naomi resisted, reminding them she had no sons left. Her words reflect the "levirate law" (*levir* means "brother-in-law"). It required a man to marry his brother's widow if he died childless; a son born of the union would bear the name and be the heir of the dead brother (see Deuteronomy 25:5-6). This preserved the family estate. We must remember that at this time the Israelites had no notion of resurrection. A man's immortality resided only in his sons and grandsons. If he died without a son, he died altogether, leaving his clan and its property holdings diminished.

But Naomi has no other sons who can marry Orpha and Ruth. Furthermore, Naomi tells them she is too old to marry again and have sons—and even if she did, the two women should not be made to wait until the sons grew up and could marry them.

Tearfully, Orpha kissed her mother-in-law good-bye, but Ruth stayed with her. It would be hard to find a more touching expression of a daughter's—in this case, a foreign daughter-in-law's—love than what Ruth says to Naomi:

> "Do not ask me to abandon or forsake you! for wherever you go I will go, wherever you lodge I will lodge; your people shall be my people, and your God my god. Wherever you die I will die, and there be buried." (1:16-17)

---

* Unless otherwise noted, Scripture citations in this chapter refer to the Book of Ruth.

Who could resist such a plea? Two women, Jew and Gentile, old and young, friend and friend, begin the long hot journey up to Jerusalem and on to Bethlehem. They arrive during the barley harvest, and the whole town is astir over them. "Naomi, back here?"

Bitterness pours up from the widow's heart:

> "Do not call me Naomi [The word means 'sweet' or 'pleasant' or even 'sweetheart.'] Call me Mara ['bitter'], for the Almighty has made it very bitter for me." (1:20)

The biblical mind: Everything, good and bad, comes from God.

How would two widows get food? Israel's law made provision for just such a need. At the harvest, workers went through the fields just once; anything they missed was left for widows, orphans and aliens to glean. And so Ruth goes to glean in an area belonging to a man named Boaz. When he comes out to the field, he notices her and, for one reason or another, becomes solicitous. He asks his workers who she is. The Moabite who came back with Naomi, they tell him (note her primary identification as "foreigner"), who has been working hard all day with scarcely a minute's rest. Boaz tells Ruth:

> "Listen, my daughter! Do not go to glean in anyone else's field....Stay here with my women servants....I have commanded the young men to do you no harm." (2:8-9)

"Why me?" Ruth asks, with the deep sense of unworthiness felt by an alien. Boaz tells her that he has heard about all she did for Naomi—how she left her own father and mother and the land of her birth to accompany her mother-in-law. At lunchtime he invites her to share his meal, and instructs his servants to let her glean where they are still harvesting—even to drop a few extra handfuls for her.

When Naomi hears all this that evening, she is delighted. She tells Ruth,

> "You would do well, my dear,...to go out with his servants; for in someone else's field you might be insulted." (2:22)

For Naomi sees hope for a solution to the problem that really troubles her: How will the seed of Elimelech enter history now that he and both his sons are dead? This Boaz is a kinsman, even though distant. He can fulfill the levirate law; he can be the *go-el* ("redeemer"), the clansman

73

who redeems his dead kinsman's name and property. And he has already shown an interest in Ruth!

But although Ruth gleans in his fields every day, when the harvest ends no proposal of marriage has been forthcoming from Boaz. If there is to be a happy ending to the story it needs the help of a wise mother-in-law, and one with imagination.

That night Naomi tells Ruth to bathe and anoint herself. When Boaz has finished the threshing and lies down after his dinner, Ruth is to lie down at his feet in a pantomimed proposal of marriage.

When Boaz awakes in the middle of the night, he is startled to find Ruth lying there.

> "Who are you?"…"I am your servant Ruth. Spread the corner of your cloak over me, for you are my next of kin." (3:9)

Boaz is immediately gallant.

> "May the LORD bless you, my daughter! You have been even more loyal now than before in not going after the young men, whether poor or rich. So be assured, daughter [Why does he keep using that word!], that I will do for you whatever you say; all my townspeople know you for a worthy woman." (3:10-11)

But a problem arises. Elimelech has a relative closer than Boaz, someone with a prior right and duty to marry Ruth! Boaz breaks the news to Ruth and sends her home with six measures of barley. But Naomi is cheerful and confident:

> "Wait here,…for the man will not rest, but will settle the matter today." (3:18)

Sure enough, Boaz hurries into the city. At its gates (where business is conducted), Boaz asks 10 city elders to sit nearby as he fulfills the law with regard to the other claimant.

He begins like a skillful lawyer, quietly announcing that Naomi wants to sell a piece of land that belonged to "our" kinsman Elimelech, her dead husband. The unnamed relative has first rights. Does he wish to press his claim?

The other man thinks quickly. Naomi is old, beyond childbearing; he can gain a field at little effort. Yes, he will press his claim. But now Boaz springs his surprise: He reveals the existence of Ruth. The kinsman will be obliged to marry her if he takes the field!

74

The bewildered kinsman faces a problem. Now there will be an extra mouth to feed—then one or two or three more. Besides, if he redeems Elimelich's property and raises up a son for him, the son will inherit the property. The kinsman will end up with less than he started with!

The kinsman takes off his sandal and hands it to Boaz to symbolize the surrender of his claim. The action rests on the fact that only the owner of a piece of property could rightfully walk on it. By the transfer of a sandal, the field and the woman are given to Boaz.

Boaz asks the elders for their witness, and we are told that *all* those at the gate, including the elders, answer:

> "We do so. May the LORD make this wife come into your house like Rachel and Leah, who between them built up the house of Israel. May you do well in Ephrathah and win fame in Bethlehem. With the offspring the LORD will give you from this girl, may your house become like the house of Perez, whom Tamar bore to Judah."
> (4:11-12)

And so they were married, and they a had a son, Obed. When Ruth's baby was born, Naomi took the child on her lap. (In the Near East, a father would take a newborn child in his lap to acknowledge it as his own.) Her neighbors rejoiced with her:

> "Blessed is the LORD who has not failed to provide you today with an heir! May he become famous in Israel! He will be your comfort and the support of your old age, for his mother is the daughter-in-law who loves you. She is worth more to you than seven sons!" (4:14-15)

And the story that began in despair ends with a great hope. Elimelech is dead, along with his sons, but thanks to the faithful love of a young widow for her mother-in-law, his seed has indeed entered history. Obed became the father of Jesse, and Jesse's son was David.

And all generations remember that Ruth, a Gentile, was one of the ancestors of Jesus.

11.
Jeremiah and Exile: The Tears of Israel

The biblical Story, as we have seen, has its ups and downs. We began
with the world's plunge downhill from Eden to Babel, then saw the
world start over in Abraham. When Abraham's descendants languished
in slavery, God sent Moses to lead them out of Egypt in the great
Exodus.

They complained in the desert and worshiped an idol; even Moses
doubted once. But God kept his word and brought his people to the
Promised Land, flowing with milk and honey. He was their only king
for a while, but he let them have mere earthly royalty when they
insisted—first Saul, a monumental failure, then David, specially
chosen and beloved, sinner and penitent, the model king who united the
tribes.

Through it all, God remained faithful—but his faithfulness
included letting his people taste the fruit of their sin, an experience
sometimes called punishment. He did his best to keep disaster at bay:

He sent *prophets* to be the conscience of Israel.

A prophet doesn't necessarily "foretell" the future. God's prophets were not sent to pass out information as to how bad the winter would be, what kind of harvest would come, when the end of the world could be expected. The word *prophet* literally means "one who speaks for God"—and the prophet speaks *in* the here and now *about* the here and now.

Some of the prophets spoke God's consolation to his people, a message of comfort after their self-induced doom had fallen on them. Others had a less pleasant task: They spoke for God in *warning*. They pointed to the future, to the inevitable consequences of Israel's actions and attitudes, but their concern was the present. They wanted people to change *now*.

Since most people don't like to be warned about anything, these prophets have generally been saddled with the title "prophets of doom." In this chapter we will try to enter the experience of one of these warning prophets.

Jeremiah has been sniffed at as a prophet of doom. He was, and it came. He and his secretary, Baruch, wrote the longest book in the Bible, spelling out the truth and its consequences. The truth was that God's people were being faithless. The consequence was the *Exile,* the bitterest milestone in Jewish history. It is, on the side of suffering, as momentous as the Exodus on the side of joy.

Power Politics

Jeremiah appears on the world stage in a scene not unlike our own: Superpowers struggling for world dominance were circling each other warily and growling, while smaller nations gambled their future on aligning themselves with the next winner. Like today's American bishops in their stand on nuclear armaments, Jeremiah ignored the "practical" political questions and addressed himself to the underlying moral issues.

In Israel, Solomon had followed David on the throne during a period of peace and prosperity, but on his death the kingdom his father had forged from a band of 12 tribes began to disintegrate. The kingdom split into two parts: Israel in the north and Judah in the south. Ten tribes clustered around a series of kings in the north (a portion of the country which includes Jesus' homeland, Galilee) with a capital at Samaria. In the south, the tribes of Judah and Benjamin retained David's throne in Jerusalem.

In the three centuries between the death of Solomon and the reign of Josiah—and the beginning of Jeremiah's career—Judah had 14 kings and one queen, every one of whom was engaged in one kind of war or another. Some introduced and encouraged false worship and coziness with pagans.

During the same period, Israel had 18 kings, mostly bad; again, their reigns were a tissue of plots, wars, invasions, idolatry. Before the time of Jeremiah—around 734 B.C.—the Assyrian king Tiglath-pileser II conquered Galilee and Transjordan. To eliminate centers of revolt, he deported influential citizens and their families to far-off areas of his empire. The land was then resettled by foreign colonists. These newcomers intermarried with those who were left behind; hence the later enmity between Jews and "half-breed" Samaritans.

Another deportation took place in 721, when the rest of Israel was conquered and its citizens deported. Men with their hands bound were marched off in columns. The women were usually not bound and could care for the needs of the prisoners. Those who could not sustain the cruel, exhausting journey were left to die. They were taken to northern Mesopotamia—that famous area between the Tigris and Euphrates rivers, modern Iraq.

A few of these deportees remained loyal to Israel's God, as we see in the instance of Tobit and his son, recorded in the book of the same name. But most succumbed to the pagan environment and were assimilated.

Thus 10 of the 12 tribes of Israel simply disappeared. It must have been an almost fatal blow to faith: the majority of God's people simply erased. (The descendants of the "lost tribes" have been variously imagined to be the Chinese, Japanese, English, American Indians, etc.—all without any proof.)

Enter the Prophet

Down south in Judah, a good king came to the throne in 640 B.C.—one without a jawbreaker name like many of the others: Josiah. The Bible records his religious reforms and mentions only in passing his daring political and military activities. He repaired the

Temple, which had become the scene of pagan worship, fertility cults and even sacred prostitution. His religious reform was the most thorough in Jewish history (and was occasioned by the discovery in 621 of a lost book of the Law—now known as Deuteronomy.)

Jeremiah was called by God just a few years earlier, 628 B.C. A member of a priestly family living a few miles from Jerusalem in a village named Anathoth, he describes God's words to him:

> Before I formed you in the womb I knew you,
>> before you were born I dedicated you,
>> a prophet to the nations I appointed you.
> "Ah Lord GOD!" I said,
>> I know not how to speak; I am too young."
> But the LORD answered me,
> Say not, "I am too young."
>> To whomever I send you, you shall go;
>> whatever I command you, you shall speak.
> Have no fear of them,
>> because I am with you to deliver you, says the LORD.
> Then the LORD extended his hand and touched my mouth, saying,
>> See, I place my words in your mouth! (Jeremiah 1:5-9*)

Jeremiah began his "speaking out for God" before Josiah's reform. His theme was always the same: God's chosen people—his bride—has been unfaithful, adulterous:

> I remember the devotion of your youth,
>> How you loved me as a bride,
> Following me in the desert,
>> in a land unsown. (2:1)

But now, "They turn to me their backs, not their faces" (2:27) and "on every high hill, under every green tree, you gave yourself to harlotry" (2:20). Sadly, God reproaches his people:

> Two evils have my people done:
>> they have forsaken me, the source of living waters;
> They have dug themselves cisterns,
>> broken cisterns, that hold no water. (2:13)

Small and great alike, all are greedy for gain;

---

* Unless otherwise noted, Scripture citations in this chapter refer to the Book of Jeremiah.

prophet and priest, all practice fraud.
They would repair, as though it were nought,
    the injury to my people:
"Peace, peace!" they say,
    though there is no peace. (6:13-14)

Jeremiah sees a "boiling cauldron that appears from the north" (1:13), the symbol of an invasion that would actually come in his lifetime. He must threaten destruction:

Up comes the lion from his lair,
    the destroyer of nations has set out,
    has left his place,
To turn your land into desolation,
    till your cities lie waste and empty. (4:7)

O daughter of my people, gird on sackcloth,
    roll in the ashes.
Mourn as for an only child
    with bitter wailing,
For sudden upon us
    comes the destroyer. (6:26)

There were "destroyers" enough around Judah. Josiah's little kingdom was surrounded by superpowers. Egypt lay to the southwest; Assyria's domination was waning in the north and east, but Babylon was becoming the new colossus of that area. As the balance of power shifted, Josiah was able to extend his military power north into the former kingdom of Israel.

Then the superpower of the south challenged the superpower of the north. Neco of Egypt moved against Babylon. He came with great waves of triremes, the battleships of the day, and landed on the Mediterranean shore of Palestine, intent on crossing the Promised Land to help failing Assyria against Babylon.

Josiah decided to stop him in the desert—probably because he wanted no revival of Assyrian power in the land he had annexed. But Josiah was disastrously defeated at the famous pass of Megiddo, the entrance to the broad plain of Esdraelon in upper Palestine, and died of his wounds shortly after. For a few months Josiah's son Jehoahaz sat on his father's throne.

When Neco the Egyptian returned south after being unsuccessful against the new Babylonian power, he replaced Josiah's first son with another and changed his name from Eliakin to Jehoiakim, indicating that he and his people were now subject to Egypt.

Deep hatred sprang up between Jeremiah and this new king. The prophet broke his plate with Jehoiakim almost immediately. The signs were clear: The reform of Josiah was over. Jeremiah's criticism was scathing. Oppression and murder were rampant in the land; the palace was being remodeled with money extorted from the poor.

Near the beginning of the new reign Jeremiah gave his famous "Temple Sermon." The people had given a superstitious and magical significance to the Temple. It was God's dwelling place; it could not possibly fall to the enemy—and, therefore, neither could the nation. Jeremiah reproved their hypocrisy:

> Hear the word of the LORD, all you of Judah who enter these gates to worship the LORD! Thus says the LORD of hosts, the God of Israel: Reform your ways and your deeds, so that I may remain with you in this place. Put not your trust in the deceitful words: "This is the temple of the LORD! The temple of the LORD! The temple of the LORD!" Only if you thoroughly reform your ways and your deeds; if each of you deals justly with his neighbors; if you no longer oppress the resident alien, the orphan, and the widow; if you no longer shed innocent blood in this place, or follow strange gods to your own harm, will I remain with you in this place, in the land which I gave your fathers long ago and forever.
>
> But here you are, putting your trust in deceitful words to your own loss! Are you to steal and murder, commit adultery and perjury, burn incense to Baal, go after strange gods that you know not, and yet come to stand before me in this house which bears my name, and say: "We are safe; we can commit all these abominations again"? Has this house which bears my name become in your eyes a den of thieves?
>
> (7:2-11)

Parables in Action

Jeremiah supported his words with certain actions which demonstrated God's warnings. He did not marry—a sort of vocation parable. Because of the terrible famine and slaughter to come, there would be no time or place to raise a family.

He took no part in mourning or festivities as a sign that none would be left to mourn and that there would be no occasion for festivities in the disastrous furture (see 16:5-8).

On one occasion he was inspired to buy a loincloth, wear it, but

not wash it. Then he hid it in a cleft of the rock. After a long interval, he went back and took it from the place where he had hidden it. It was rotted, good for nothing. Then the message:

> "Thus says the LORD: 'So also will I allow the pride of Judah to rot, the great pride of Jerusalem.'" (13:9)

On another occasion, Jeremiah brought a potter's earthen flask. Then he took some of the elders and priests to the Valley of Hinnom—the deep valley south of Jersulaem which, because of its endless burning fires (it was a city dump), Jesus compared to eternal punishment. There Jeremiah accused them of all their sins—adoring strange gods, child sacrifice, the shedding of innocent blood, worship of Baal.

Therefore God would punish the city. As a sign of this Jeremiah broke the flask in the sight of his companions and said:

> "Thus says the LORD of hosts: 'Thus will I smash this people and this city as one smashes a clay pot so that it cannot be repaired.'" (19:10)

This was too much. The priest Pashur, son of the chief officer of the Temple, had him scourged and placed in the stocks at one of the city gates. He was released the next morning.

Jeremiah's Dark Night

Jeremiah didn't like what he said any better than the rulers and priests. He tells us more about his inner feelings than perhaps any other figure in the Old Testament. One of his remarkable self-revelations follows the account of his imprisonment. Being a prophet of doom is not only an unpleasant task, it is not even what Jeremiah signed up for—or so he tells us. He had been promised that he would "build and plant" as well as "destroy and demolish" (see 1:1), and he is tired of paying the penalty for offering king and people bitter wine to drink. Is there ever going to be a time for building and planting, he wonders?

He has already dared to call God a "treacherous brook" that dries up when its waters are needed (see 15:18), but now he goes even further. A cry of bitterness rises from Jeremiah's heart: He has been seduced! Yet even as he spews out his anger at God, the strong current of trust and dedication can still be heard:

> You duped me, O LORD, and I let myself be duped;

You were too strong for me, and you triumphed.
All the day I am an object of laughter;
    everyone mocks me.
Whenever I speak, I must cry out,
    violence and outrage is my message;
The word of the LORD has brought me
    derision and reproach all the day.
I say to myself, I will not mention him,
    I will speak in his name no more.
But then it becomes like fire burning in my heart,
    imprisoned in my bones;
I grow weary holding it in,
    I cannot endure it.
Yes, I hear the whisperings of many:
    "Terror on every side!
    Denounce! let us denounce him!"
All those who were my friends
    are on the watch for any misstep of mine.
"Perhaps he will be trapped; then we can prevail,
    and take our vengeance on him."
But the LORD is with me, like a mighty champion:
    my persecutors will stumble, they will not triumph.
In their failure they will be put to utter shame,
    to lasting, unforgettable confusion. (20:7-11)

A Letter of Consolation

This prophet of doom has one chance to speak of better days to come. Jeremiah writes to those who are already in exile—the worst was yet to come in 587 B.C.—telling them to settle down and lead a normal life. The Exile will last 70 years. *But God will save his people:*

For thus says the LORD:
Shout with joy for Jacob,
    exult at the head of the nations;
    proclaim your praise and say:
The LORD has delivered his people,
    the remnant of Israel.
Behold, I will bring them back
    from the land of the north;
I will gather them from the ends of the world,
    with the blind and the lame in their midst,
The mothers and those with child;
    they shall return as an immense throng.
They departed in tears,

但 I will console them and guide them;
I will lead them to brooks of waters,
   on a level road, so that none shall stumble.
For I am a father to Israel,
   Ephraim is my first-born. (31:7-9)

Tragedy in the South

But the end of the Jews' suffering has not yet come. Now the south, Jeremiah's land, was to be caught in the clash of empires. In 597 the Babylonian king Nebuchadnezzar deported Judah's king and the royal family, the nobles, the warriors and the artisans—perhaps 7,000 to 10,000 people—Exodus in reverse.

The conqueror put a new king on the throne, Zedekiah. Understandably, an underground arose, plotting to throw off the Babylonian yoke.

Now, like all prophets, Jeremiah gets into "politics." The God who directs history has allowed Babylon to conquer Judah so that his people will remember him again. Resistance to God's action can only lead to further disaster.

Jeremiah performs another parable-in-action, walking the streets of Jerusalem wearing a wooden yoke and saying:

> Submit your necks to the yoke of the king of Babylon; serve him and his people, so that you may live. Why should you and your people die by sword, famine, and pestilence, with which the LORD has threatened the nation that will not serve the king of Babylon?
>
> (27:12-14)

A rival prophet, Hananiah, took the yoke from Jeremiah's neck and broke it, promising the people that they would throw off the invader's yoke in two years. Jeremiah responded that they were forging an iron yoke for themselves.

The endless clash of empires continued. In 601 B.C. Egypt seemed to be coming to Israel's aid against the occupying Babylonians. But Jeremiah sent this word from the Lord to the hopeful King Zedekiah:

> Pharaoh's army which has set out to help you will return to its own land. The Chaldeans [Babylonians] shall return to the fight against this city [Jerusalem]; they shall capture it and destroy it with fire.
>
> (37:7-8)

This time it seemed the prophet was wrong. The Chaldeans

withdrew at the Egyptian threat. Jeremiah took the occasion to visit his hometown of Anathoth near Jerusalem, but when he reached the Gate of Benjamin, he was accused of trying to desert. The authorities had him beaten and thrown into prison where he stayed "a long time" (37:16). Ultimately he was transferred to a relaxed house arrest.

Jeremiah continued his sad warnings. Those who would go out to join the Chaldeans would live, those who remained in the city would die by the sword. But the prudent thing, the royal court saw, was to ally with Egypt. The princes complained to the king about Jeremiah:

> "This man ought to be put to death,...he demoralizes the soliders who are left in the city, and all the people, by speaking such things to them; he is not interested in the welfare of our people, but in their ruin." (38:4)

Pilate-like, the king gave in. They took Jeremiah and threw him into an empty cistern. Jeremiah sank into the mud at the bottom—but his friend Ebed-melech arranged his rescue.

Disaster

Finally the Egyptians withdrew and the Babylonians returned to the siege of Jerusalem. The walls were breached in the summer of 587 B.C. The king was captured, forced to watch the execution of his sons, and then blinded. The city was burned and the Temple destroyed. Judah seems to have become merely a province of Samaria. Surrounding nations moved in to pillage and occupy.

Again a sad line of deportees trudged away from their homeland. This time they were relocated in southern Mesopotamia. Among the places, strangely, was Tel-Aviv, southeast of the great city of Babylon.

They lived a fairly normal life as slave labor for the building projects of Nebuchadnezzar—less a concentration camp existence than a liberal internment. Some, in fact, prospered so well that they or their children did not want to leave after the 50-year Exile. Some fell into the paganism surrounding them.

In devastated Jerusalem and its environs, a pitiful remnant of vinedressers and plowmen remained. It was not yet the deeply religious "remnant" which another prophet, Isaiah, said the Lord would use to rebuild his people.

Jeremiah was one who stayed behind. At first he found himself among captives about to be deported to Babylon. The captain of the guard, however, allowed him to remain.

Again political machinations rose among the people. Some had an itch to go to Egypt. They asked Jeremiah to consult the Lord. The answer came: They were to remain with the conquerors.

> "If you remain quietly in this land I will build you up...for I regret the evil I have done you." (42:10)

Nevertheless, a group did leave. Jeremiah went along—whether willingly or unwillingly we do not know. Nothing is known of his death in Egypt. A tradition known only through Christian writings says he was stoned to death in Tahpanhes.

His last days must have been terribly sad. His country—the land which the Lord had so graciously prepared for his people—lay in ruins. The beginning to another biblical book describes its plight:

> How lonely she is now,
>   the once crowded city!
> Widowed is she
>   who was mistress over nations;
> The princess among the provinces
>   has been made a toiling slave.
> Bitterly she weeps at night,
>   tears upon her cheeks,
> With not one to console her
>   of all her dear ones;
> Her friends have all betrayed her
>   and become her enemies. (Lamentations 1:1-2)

Singing of Yahweh in a Strange Land

From every viewpoint but one, the Exile was a total disaster, a practically total disintegration of all God had built up from the time of Abraham. The Jews faced the same crisis of faith they would later face at Auschwitz: Is God with us, or not?

From the viewpoint of faith, the biblical mentality, there was an explanation. When God's people become independent—the sin of Paradise—he lets them have their self-sufficiency. They sink, like Peter trying to walk on the water. When they are drowning in helplessness, they know again their need for God, and they let him lift them up again.

The Exile had some good results. It produced a sadder, wiser people. The Temple with its magnificent liturgies was gone. Gradually the Jews realized they may have placed too much emphasis on sacrificing to God *only* at Jerusalem, in the Temple. God was one, and he was everywhere. In the pain of exile they came to know their God more deeply, and their faith was forged in that fire. Gradually they reconciled themselves to the situation; the Book (the Torah or Pentateuch, the first five books of our Bible), the sabbath, and circumcision became their source of unity. It is possible that the synagogue first made its appearance during the Exile as a substitute for Temple worship.

It will give us an added insight in reading the Bible to know that scholars believe much work went into the sacred books during the Exile. Most of the historical books were collected and edited at that time. The same is true of much of prophetic literature, and two major prophetic works, Ezekiel and Second Isaiah (Isaiah 40—55, the beautiful "Book of Consolation") were written then.

In that spirit, we have saved the most hopeful words of Jeremiah till last. To the Jews in Exile, they must have been candles of hope against the darkness; to Christians this passage is known as "the gospel before the gospel":

> The days are coming, says the LORD, when I will make a new covenant with the house of Israel and the house of Judah. It will not be like the covenant I made with their fathers the day I took them by the hand to lead them forth from the land of Egypt; for they broke my covenant and I had to show myself their master, says the LORD. But this is the covenant which I will make with the house of Israel after those days, says the LORD. I place my law within them, and write it upon their hearts; I will be their God, and they shall be my people. No longer will they have need to teach their friends and kinsmen how to know the LORD. All, from least to greatest, shall know me, says the LORD, for I will forgive their evildoing and remember their sin no more. (31:31-34)

12.
Daniel: A Hero for the Underground

Suppose an anonymous writer in today's Poland wanted to encourage Solidarity members to persevere in their cause. Writing about Lech Walesa would be too obvious; the writer would quickly attract the attention of the authorities. So instead he creates a fictional hero and places him in conflict with the tyrants of another age—say when Poland was under the heel of the Austrians or the Prussians. Solidarity members will understand exactly what the writer is saying, but the authorities have no grounds to object.

A farfetched idea? Not at all. The French dramatist Anouilh did just that with his "Greek" play *Antigone* during the Nazi occupation of France. So did an unknown Jewish writer who composed the Book of Daniel about 164 B.C. He created a character named Daniel and placed his story in the Babylonian captivity over four centuries earlier.

In those four centuries, empires rose and fell—and the fortunes of the Jews with them. The Babylonian conquerors who set the Jews trudging into exile fell before the Medes who succumbed to Persia; it was the Persian king Cyrus whose edict of religious freedom made it possible for the Jews to return to Jerusalem and rebuild the Temple. Then the Greeks took their turn on the stage of history, peaking with Alexander's conquest of all the known world and, after his death, disintegrating into four small kingdoms.

In these centuries the Jews had many rulers—some benevolent, some harsh. But in 175 B.C. a vicious Greek king named Antiochus IV, with the sufferance of Rome, took over royal power. He is described by John McKenzie as "eccentric and capricious, mingling with the crowds in revelry and carelessly distributing huge sums of money, capable of barbaric cruelty" *(Dictionary of the Bible,* p. 37).

Satire always nails the pompous. Antiochus gave himself the name Epiphanes, "the manifestation of Zeus himself." The name, pronounced "Epiphaneez," soon became in popular parlance *Epimaneez—*"the madman."

Even before Antiochus came to power, there had been a movement (Hellenization) toward adoption of Greek customs and abandonment of Israel's religious and cultural traditions, but the majority of Jews had resisted. Now Antiochus attempted to force the acceptance of Greek religion and culture. He empowered his army to suppress Jewish worship, sacred books and religious practices, and to introduce the worship of Greek gods. The last straw was the erection of an altar to Zeus in the Temple—the "abomination of desolation" described in the Book of Daniel. (The phrase came to be a common description of any violation of the holy by godless powers; Jesus used it in Matthew 24:15.) *When you see the desolating abomination ... those in Judea must flee to the mountains*

This period of persecution finally led to an actual revolt which is described in the last historical books of the Old Testament, 1 and 2 Maccabees. But first a resistance literature—our concern for this chapter—developed.

The Book of Daniel was meant to encourage those suffering under the heel of tyrants. The book does not advocate revolt. It rests in the absolute hope that God will someday accomplish his own revolution and save his people.

The book is divided into two major parts. It begins with *six edifying stories* about the hero, Daniel, and his three companions in the royal court of Babylon during the Exile.

92

In the second part Daniel has *four visions* in which he beholds, in highly symbolic images, God working in history to establish his own Kingdom. This part introduces us to a form of biblical writing called *apocalyptic,* which will be discussed below.

Finally, three more stories about Daniel appear in an *appendix*. Orginially written in Greek, this last section has never been included in the Jewish Scriptures. It probably indicates that many Daniel stories circulated in Israel at the time of Antiochus' persecutions.

The Stories

As the *Jerome Biblical Commentary* notes, "we have no way of knowing whether the Daniel of these stories was really an historical character, about whom popular legends gradually clustered, or whether he was simply a creation of Jewish folklore" (p. 448). But it doesn't matter. We must again remember that the Bible is a faith-book. In both historical and fictionalized accounts it is a faith view of the relationship of God and his people.

The purpose of the Daniel stories is to inculcate a moral lesson. Daniel is a model of wisdom, courage and fidelity. He is a hero to the second-century Jews for what he did in the days of Exile. If we take a look at the six stories which begin this book, the message is clear.

1) *God and the Vegetable Diet*. When Pope Paul VI abrogated the Church law of Friday abstinence a few years ago, many Catholics were dismayed and scandalized. Not eating meat on Friday had become a *symbol* of Catholic identity, a way all the world could see they were different from other people—even from other Christians. The question of Friday's menu was not the *substance* of the quarrel that divided Catholics and Protestants, but it was the most obvious everyday mark of allegiance to the Church of Rome.

At the time the Book of Daniel was written the dietary laws of the Bible were the "Friday abstinence" symbol for the Jews. *Pork* was a Gentile food and a symbol of Gentile values; abstinence from pork became the touchstone of orthodox Judaism.

We first meet Daniel and his three companions at the Babylonian court. The king, Nebuchadnezzar, wants some Israelites in his service, young men

of royal blood and of the nobility....without any defect, handsome,

> intelligent and wise, quick to learn, and prudent in judgment.
>
> (Daniel 1:3-4*)

But Daniel and the three would not defile themselves with the food and wine from the king's table—Gentile food, Gentile values. So Daniel struck a pact with the king's steward: They would have nothing but vegetables and water for 10 days; then a comparison would be made with those who had eaten of the king's menu. The result: After 10 days they looked healthier and better fed than any of the young men who ate from the royal table (see 1:15).

So the second-century Jews are encouraged to resist the Hellenization Antiochus is trying to impose. Remember, this book says, God preserves those who keep their heritage pure.

2) *The Dream of King Nebuchadnezzar*. The second story anticipates the second half of the Book of Daniel. God will ultimately establish his own Kingdom, it says to the persecuted Jews: Don't lose hope.

Nebuchadnezzar had a dream, and his own astrologers and soothsayers were unable to interpret it. Daniel volunteers to explain it. He does so—a sign of the superiority of Israel's God-given wisdom over the worldly wisdom of the pagans. The king had to admit, "Truly your God is the God of gods and the Lord of kings" (2:47), and he advanced Daniel to a high post.

The dream went like this: Nebuchadnezzar saw a giant statue. The head was gold, the chest and arms were silver. Belly and thighs were bronze, the legs were iron, the feet partly iron, partly clay tile. A huge stone, hewn from a mountain—but not by human hands—struck the feet, breaking them. Then the whole statue crumbled at once, fine as chaff, and was blown away by the wind. The stone became a great mountain which filled the whole earth.

Daniel's interpretation was that the four metals stood for four kingdoms: Nebuchadnezzar's Babylonians (the gold) would be conquered by the Medes (the silver) who in turn would be taken over by the Persians (the bronze) until, finally, the Greeks—the *iron* hand now persecuting the Jews—would come to power. The author is bringing past history up to date by letting his hero predict the future.

---

* Unless otherwise noted, Scripture citations in this chapter refer to the Book of Daniel.

Through all this, it is God who "causes the changes of the times and the seasons" (2:21). God is the Lord of history. He makes kings and unmakes them, and he will lead human history to the conclusion he has designed for it, in spite of and through the free will of his children. God will "set up a kingdom that shall never be destroyed" (2:44).

So, second-century persecuted Jews: Don't give up! Ultimately we will inherit God's Kingdom. We shall overcome!

3) *The Fiery Furnace.* This story still lives in the lilting spiritual about Shadrach, Mishach and Abednego. Here Daniel yields the spotlight to the three young men who were his companions in the first story.

Nebuchadnezzar, apparently forgetting his recognition of the God of the Jews, erected a statue 90 feet high and required everyone to worship his pagan god. These three Jewish men, now provincial administrators, were reported to the king as being disobedient. He flew into a rage, hailed them before him and threatened to throw them into a white-hot fire unless they worshiped the statue. Their reply:

> "If our God, whom we serve, can save us from the white-hot furnace and from your hands, O king, may he save us! But if he will not, know, O king, that we will not serve your god or worship the golden statue which you set up." (3:17-18)

An act of trust for all seasons, Exile to Auschwitz.

The King's men stoked the furnace with brimstone, pitch, tow and wood; the flames rose over 70 feet. But the angel of the Lord went down into the furnace with the three youths and kept them safe.

"Blessed are you!" the young men shouted in the prayer of praise which the Church often uses in the liturgy today, the "blessing song" (3:52-90).

The king was amazed when the youths emerged without even the smell of fire on their clothing. Again he blessed the God of Israel:

> "[T]here is no other God who can rescue like this." (3:96)

So, second-century persecuted Jews: Don't give up! Your exile may seem as bad as a fiery furnace, but God will rescue his people in his own time. Even if it seems he never will do this, trust!

4) *The Writing on the Wall.* Now we have a new Babylonian king, Belshazzar, but the same wise Daniel who is about to interpret the

actions of God—and who therefore stands as an assurance to persecuted Jews that the wisdom and power of God still sustains them.

Belshazzar had a great feast for a thousand of his lords and their wives. He brought in the gold and silver vessels which his father had stolen from the Temple of Jerusalem. The festivities were interrupted when a hand appeared and wrote three cryptic words on the wall. When none of the king's wise men could interpret them, Daniel was called.

The three words—*mene, tekel, peres*—literally seem to have been the names of weights or coins. But Daniel interpreted them by a play on words, interpreting *mene* as "to number," *tekel* "to weigh," and *peres* "to divide":

> "MENE, God has numbered your kingdom and put an end to it;
> TEKEL, you have been weighed on the scales and found wanting;
> PERES, your kingdom has been divided and given to the Medes and the Persians." (5:26-27)

Strangely, in the face of such bad news, Belshazzar clothed Daniel in purple and made him third in the kingdom.

So, second-century Jews under another king who has desecrated the Temple: God will punish those who lay sacrilegious hands on his people and on their Temple and its sacred vessels.

5) *Daniel in the Lions' Den*. Babylon fell to the Persians and Daniel rose in the service of a new king, Darius. Envy at Daniel's success prompted lower government officials (unable to accuse him of any real fault) to flatter the king into putting a phony law into force: For 30 days no one is to address any petition to god or man—only to the king. Anyone violating this law would be thrown into a den of lions.

Of course Daniel—model of faithful prayer and service to God—continued his custom of kneeling in prayer three times a day, gazing out the window toward far-off Jerusalem.

Now the envious had their case against Daniel, and he was thrown into the lions' den. With his own ring, the king sealed the stone which was brought to block the opening of the den.

Like Pilate later, the king was a reluctant participant in the crime; he could not sleep. He went to the den, crying out to the supposedly dead Daniel.

But Daniel's voice came clear in the dawn:

"My God has sent his angel and closed the lions' mouths so that they have not hurt me."...Daniel was removed from the den, *unhurt because he trusted in his God*. (6:23-24, emphasis added)

Once more the message is clear to second-century Jews: Trust.

The Visions of Daniel

We come now to a style of writing that has caused endless speculation and massive misinterpretation in both New and Old Testaments, especially in the Book of Revelation and in some of Jesus' words. It is called *apocalypse* literature, and it was in vogue from 200 B.C. to 200 A.D. The word *apocalypse* means "revelation" and revelation is its formula: Heavenly secrets about a cosmic struggle between God's forces and the forces of evil are revealed to a seer in such highly *symbolic* form they have to be explained by angels. Often the writer is supposedly living centuries before: The vision is sometimes attributed to a famous personage of the past, such as Moses. The reader, of course, knows this "future" has already happened.

But apocalyptic writing also sees a real future in which God will finally crash into history with a terrible vindication of the good who have been persecuted by the powers of evil.

The purpose of this "underground" or "resistance" writing was to enable the persecuted Jews to cope with the existing order rather than to change it: God will take care of that, someday, in an explosive intervention into the world. The author wants to convey wisdom and understanding: The world is a vast theater of conflicting supernatural forces, but a glorious end for the just is guaranteed. Hang on!

The scene of apocalyptic writing is this cosmic struggle between supernatural forces—good and evil. Daniel no longer associates comfortably with the Nebuchadnezzars and Belshazzars of this world. Now all kingdoms are the enemy (summed up, as it were, in Antiochus Epiphanes, the persecutor against whom this book was written). Only the direct action of God can transform the world into a new order. The Gentile kingdoms cannot be reformed; they can only be destroyed. Then will come the worldwide reign of God.

We will consider here just one of the four visions of Daniel. Narrated in Chapter 7, it is the vision most often presented in Christian liturgy, and it is one of the most powerful scenes in the Bible.

In Daniel's terrifying dream, winds from the four corners of the earth stir up the great sea—the abyss of Genesis which God once controlled and put in order. That abyss is the abode of chaos and monsters, the headquarters of evil. Four beasts rise from the murky waters, representing the four kingdoms which have tyrannized the Jews over the past centuries (see pp. 91-92).

The *lion* is Babylon (its two "plucked" wings Nebuchadnezzar and Belshazzar)—a beastly power hostile to God and to his people.

The *bear* with three fangs, destined to "devour much flesh," is the kingdom of the Medes.

The *leopard* is Persia; its four heads and four wings symbolize its kings: Cyrus, Xerxes, Artaxerxes and Darius.

Too terrible to be compared to any known beast are the *Greeks*, now grinding the people down in the persecution of Antiochus. The 10 horns stand for 10 rulers up to the writer's time; the "little horn" which springs up separately calls further attention to the current tyrant.

Then comes the vision of the heavenly court:

> Thrones were set up
>> and the Ancient One took his throne.
> His clothing was snow bright,
>> and the hair on his head as white as wool;
> His throne was flames of fire,
>> with wheels of burning fire.
> A surging stream of fire
>> flowed out from where he sat;
> Thousands upon thousands were ministering to him,
> and myriads upon myriads attended him. (7:9-10)

The Ancient of Days is God. The description of his throne owes something to the famous description in Ezekiel 1. It is a scene of splendor and awe, with a touch of fear to compare with the vision of the beasts.

The beasts are defeated, and as the vision continued, Daniel saw:

> One like a son of man* coming,
>> on the clouds of heaven;
> When he reached the Ancient One
>> and was presented before him,
> he received dominion, glory, and kingship:
> nations and peoples of every language serve him.
> His dominion is an everlasting dominion
>> that shall not be taken away,

98

his kingship shall not be destroyed. (7:13-14)

This is one of the key passages of the Bible, adding a new dimension of hope to the promise God gave to David (see p. 68). The *Jerome Biblical Commentary* offers this explanation:

> The son of man is a figure of the kingdom of the "holy ones of the Most High" (v. 18). In the context, therefore, the son of man is not a real individual but a figure of speech. However, because in Daniel the thought of "kingdom" often shifts imperceptibly into that of "king," the concept of the "son of man" gradually shifted...into a term for the messianic king himself. (p. 356)

The Message of Daniel

From the suffering of the Jews under a cruel persecutor, the Book of Daniel has moved to a vision of cosmic evil, greater than its individual manifestations. Like the terrifying chaos at the beginning, all the forces of evil—Antiochus, Caesar, Stalin, Hitler—hint at a great evil that lies behind, silent and insatiable.

So also there is a Goodness. It is silent, life-giving, omnipotent. It lies behind the trust and long-suffering of God's people. The just may not have earthly success. But they will shine like stars forever.

God will triumph.

The Kingdom will come.

Blessèd are those who hope....

---

* As an individual Hebrew expression, the term "son of man" means an *individual* as contrasted to *adam,* humankind. It can also mean the heavenly figure mentioned by Daniel, who will appear at the end of time, or represent the holy ones of the Most High, the redeemed community.

In the Gospels only Jesus uses the phrase, and he uses it to refer to himself. Jesus uses the phrase to describe his earthly activity, his suffering and resurrection, and his future end-time action. It is important to remember that Jesus combined the concept of the son of man with that of the humble and suffering Servant of Isaiah (see Isaiah 42:1-4; 49: 1-7; 50:4-11; 52:13—53:12).

13.
Mary, the Flowering of Israel's Faith: An Epilogue

Let's say it once more: The Bible is a *faith*-book. It was written by people who looked back over their history and saw God at work there. *How* God worked was always less important than *what* he did, so they didn't pay very careful attention to the details when they retold their stories.

Israel's Story is our Story. We see the Old Testament from the vantage point of our own history. To us it seems to look forward to the wonderful thing God did for us in Jesus. The story of Jesus is the story Christians can never stop retelling; it has been embroidered by poets and storytellers from the first Gospel-writers down to our own day because here, too, the details of how God works are less important than what God does.

In that spirit, I offer here a small story about a young woman who was nurtured on the biblical stories, in the biblical faith. It is pure fiction—and absolutely true.

101

The Flowering of Israel's Faith

The dawn was barely tinting the narrow street as she left the house, carrying a water jar. She strode vigorously, eager for the new day. She was tall, now fully a woman. Her black hair was gathered at the back of her neck with a yellow band. Her chin and mouth were firm, her eyes wide and alert, as if expecting a surprise around each corner.

Where she reached the well, she saw Rebecca, slumped on the ground against the low stone wall, her shawl almost hiding her face.

Rebecca recognized the bare feet and dress as the woman lowered her jar into the well. At least there would be no contempt.

The woman took the jar from the rope and set it on the edge of the well.

"How are you, Rebecca?"

For a moment, the huddled figure on the ground turned away, as if to grind itself into the dust. Then she rolled over suddenly and threw herself at the feet of the woman. Sobs shook her body, and the tears began to fall on the woman's feet.

The woman sat down and lifted Rebecca's arms. They embraced each other tightly, Rebecca sobbing, the woman softly whispering and patting her back as a mother comforts her baby.

Rebecca's head slid down onto the woman's lap. The sobbing began to subside. There was a long silence, as the woman stroked her hair.

Barely a whisper.

"I was with Chaim again last night. I am worthless. I am filthy. My husband—"

"Rebecca, God forgives. You are not worthless to him. Don't give up. Today is a new day." She lifted her until they could look into each other's eyes.

After a while they rose and brushed the dust from their dresses.

"Go home now, Rebecca. Bathe yourself, fix your hair, make a meal. Your husband loves you."

The woman watched her walk away, slowly at first, her shoulders carrying her life. Then she turned around and smiled. She threw back her shawl and went into the awakening town.

The woman left her jar at the well and walked down the hill to a grassy spot near a plane tree. She sat down, let her head rest back